A Union of Diversities

A Union of Diversities

Style in the Music of Charles Ives

LARRY STARR

SCHIRMER BOOKS
A Division of Macmillan, Inc.
NEW YORK

Maxwell Macmillan Canada
TORONTO

Maxwell Macmillan International
NEW YORK   OXFORD   SINGAPORE   SYDNEY

Copyright © 1992 by Schirmer Books
A Division of Macmillan, Inc.

Schirmer Books
A Division of Macmillan, Inc.
866 Third Avenue
New York, NY 10022

#23940447

Maxwell Macmillan Canada, Inc.
1200 Eglinton Avenue East, Suite 200
Don Mills, Ontario M3C 3N1

Macmillan, Inc. is part of the Maxwell
Communication Group of Companies

Library of Congress Catalog Card Number: 91–22486

Printed in the United States of America

printing number
1 2 3 4 5 6 7 8 9 10

Library of Congress Cataloging-in-Publication Data

Starr, Larry.
    A union of diversities : style in the music of Charles Ives / by
Larry Starr.
        p.   cm.
    Includes index.
    ISBN 0–02–872465–8
    1. Ives, Charles, 1874–1954—Criticism and interpretation.
2. Style, Musical.   I. Title.
ML410.I94S7   1992
780'.92—dc20   91–22486
                                                            CIP
                                                            MN

The paper used in this publication meets the minimum requirements of
American National Standard for Information Sciences—Permanence
of Paper for Printed Library Materials. ANSI Z39.48–1984.

Contents

Preface

My book is an exploration of the unique musical experiences offered by the work of Charles Ives. Unlike all other books on Ives, this one is devoted exclusively to the understanding and appreciation of Ives's music itself, from the perspective of the *listener*. Unlike other literature dealing with the analysis of Ives's music, this book is designed to be as accessible as possible to any reader with an interest in Ives's work, regardless of whether that reader possesses an extensive musical background. My goal of maximum accessibility has involved not the slightest compromise in the book's musical or intellectual content. On the contrary, it has become clear to me from my own study of Ives that the wider the audience addressed in these pages, and the freer these pages are of professional jargon, the closer they may come to the true spirit and meaning of his work.

Ives's life and times, and the cultural and philosophical milieu in which he worked, have already been studied extensively and well, which is one reason why I do not deal with them here. Another reason is that Ives's music can appeal and make sense, to a surprising degree, without detailed reference to the circumstances of its origin. Knowing about the composer and his background assuredly can stimulate deepened interest in, and insight into, his music. But the reverse proposition is also true, and this book offers readers the opportunity to approach Ives first, and primarily, through his music, as it is experienced in our own time.

Thus, these pages will not reiterate biographical and other general information about Ives and his career, which is readily available elsewhere, except for occasional points that are immediately germane to the musical experience at hand. One of my goals in writing this book is to encourage readers unfamiliar with such information to seek it out, demonstrating through Ives's music that such information should be interesting and important to them.

A Bibliographical Note

There are two fine introductory books about Charles Ives. *Charles Ives and His Music* by Henry and Sidney Cowell is a pioneering work on the composer, written while he was still alive, and it remains of unique value for its insights into Ives as man and musician. The most recent edition (New York: Da Capo, 1983) is a reprint of the second (1969) edition. H. Wiley Hitchcock's *Ives* (London: Oxford University Press, 1977) emphasizes the music, summarizing Ives's contributions to various genres and discussing a number of works in detail.

Biographical material about Ives, both of a documentary and an interpretive nature, is abundant. Again, I will call the reader's attention to two essential volumes. Vivian Perlis's *Charles Ives Remembered: An Oral History* (New Haven and London: Yale University Press, 1974) is a collection of important and fascinating interviews with family, friends, business associates, and musicians who knew Ives. The most recent book-length biographical study is Frank R. Rossiter's *Charles Ives and His America* (New York: Liveright, 1975).

Critical studies of the composer with varying emphases have appeared. Among them are Rosalie Sandra Perry's ambitiously titled *Charles Ives and the American Mind* (Kent, Ohio: Kent State University Press, 1974), which is rather general concerning Ives's music, and most recently, J. Peter Burkholder's *Charles Ives: The Ideas Behind the Music* (New Haven and London: Yale University Press, 1985), a most substantial exegesis of the development of Ives's aesthetic thought. An additional volume by Burkholder, applying his findings to detailed study of the music, is eagerly anticipated. A collection of scholarly papers on various facets of Ives and his work is *An Ives Celebration,* edited by H. Wiley Hitchcock and Vivian Perlis (Urbana: University of Illinois Press, 1977).

Major current issues in Ives scholarship are the dating and chronology of his works, and the formal and "psychological" analysis of his music based on the employment of musical quotations. Dating and chronology is the focus of Maynard Solomon's controversial article "Charles Ives: Some Questions of Veracity," *Journal of the American Musicological Society* Vol. 40, No. 3 (Fall 1987): pp. 443–470. Carol K. Baron's "Dating Charles Ives's Music: Facts and Fictions," *Perspectives of New Music* Vol. 28, No. 1 (Winter 1990): pp. 20–56, offers a rebuttal to Solomon and opens up additional important issues. For formal analysis based on the use of quotations, see especially J. Peter Burkholder's " 'Quotation' and Emulation: Charles Ives's Uses of His Models," *The Musical Quarterly* Vol. 71, No. 1 (1985): pp. 1–26. For an example of "psychological" analysis based on the use of quotations, see Stuart Feder's "The Nostalgia of Charles Ives: An Essay in Affects and Music," *The Annual of Psychoanalysis* Vol. 10 (1982): pp. 301–332.

Geoffrey Block's *Charles Ives: A Bio-Bibliography* (New York: Greenwood, 1988) is an invaluable annotated guide to all this literature and to just about everything else of any relevance to the study of Ives. It includes a thorough discography, a list of works and performances, and many other features of great interest to anyone concerned with this composer.

At the moment, the study of Ives may be in a paradoxically better condition than much of the man's music itself. Ives never prepared the vast majority of his output for formal publication, and left the bulk of his work in disarray, which is only beginning to be seriously resolved. The Charles Ives Society was formed in 1973 to support the creation and publication of reliable scholarly-critical editions of Ives's works. The Society's offices are at the Institute for Studies in American Music, Brooklyn College, CUNY, and dependable published scores of Ives's music are at last appearing under their auspices.

Acknowledgments

The conception and execution of this book are products of the author's own ideas and labor. The errors, flaws, and limitations of this work should consequently be laid at nobody's doorstep but my own. I would like, however, to thank those who have encouraged my work and who have helped me find ways to control my shortcomings.

I owe sincere thanks to the Editor-in-Chief at Schirmer Books, Maribeth Anderson Payne, who believed in this project from the beginning and who has offered me much valuable advice throughout its gestation. I wish to acknowledge also the valuable contributions of Robert J. Axelrod, Associate Editor at Schirmer Books. To those readers (unknown to me) who carefully scrutinized the manuscript for Schirmer Books in various stages of its completion, I extend my deep gratitude; this project underwent much clarification and improvement as a result of their suggestions and, even in cases where their suggestions were not taken, I found it useful and important to consider them. My particular thanks go to Denise Cooney, an Ives scholar-to-be, whose interest in this manuscript and whose reactions to it have been very significant and helpful to me at all stages of my work. To the publishers of Ives's music, who have graciously granted permission to reprint substantial excerpts and even complete songs, I must also offer my thanks; this book would be much less useful to the reader without these extensive musical examples.

The University of Washington was most generous in awarding both summer salary and sabbatical leave to support me when this book was in its crucial formative stages. I thank my institutional "home" for this and many other ways in which my scholarly work has been encouraged and aided.

This book is dedicated, first to my parents, who led me to love music and to look for enduring values in both art and life experiences; to my wife Leslie and to my children Dan, Sonya, and Gregory, who believe in me and in what I do, and from whom I learn so much every day; to my students, who always teach me much more than I can ever return to them; and finally, and reverently, to the memory of Charles Ives, whose work has enriched my own life, and the lives of so many others, immeasurably.

L. S.

A Union of Diversities

. . . a song has a *few* rights, the same as other ordinary citizens. If it feels like walking along the left-hand side of the street, passing the door of physiology or sitting on the curb, why not let it? If it feels like kicking over an ash can, a poet's castle, or the prosodic law, will you stop it? . . . Should it not have a chance to sing to itself, if it can sing?—to enjoy itself without making a bow, if it can't make a bow?—to swim around in any ocean, if it can swim, without having to swallow "hook and bait," or being sunk by an operatic greyhound? If it happens to feel like trying to fly where humans cannot fly, to sing what cannot be sung, to walk in a cave on all fours, or to tighten up its girth in blind hope and faith and try to scale mountains that are not, who shall stop it?

—In short, must a song always be a song!

—*Charles Ives,*
from the postface to 114 Songs

Prelude

An unconventional man demands an unconventional book.

I offer here a book on the music of Charles Ives, based upon deeply-felt convictions that might initially strike the reader as unusual. I state these convictions directly at the outset, to make it clear what this book is and is not attempting to do. I hope that the discussions, analyses, and even digressions constituting the main body of this work will be seen to justify, at least in part, the convictions upon which they have been based.

My first and central conviction is that Charles Ives, certainly a special, and purportedly a "difficult," composer, need not be a specialist's composer. Ives, in fact, had little use for music specialists, and addressed his music to an idealized audience comprised not of specialists—of any stripe—but of "Everyman" and "Everywoman." This book is therefore addressed not primarily to Ives specialists (although I hope they will find some things of interest in it) or even solely to music professionals, but to any interested music lover who has the curiosity to approach Ives's music and the willingness to approach that music directly, patiently, and without preconceptions. My analyses are intended to be accessible to all who can follow standard concert program notes or the descriptive material that usually accompanies discs or tapes of concert music. References to musical notation in the text are designed to be within the grasp of anyone who has sung in a choir or has endured the rite-of-passage of childhood music lessons. I have strived to use only those musical terms that are clearly defined in a basic college dictionary.

I hasten to assure specialists that my desire to produce a book accessible to the widest possible range of readers has not resulted at any point in oversimplification. This is because Ives's essential musical communication may be grasped, meaningfully and deeply, by music lovers on all levels of training and experience. Moreover, the *most* important things Ives has to communicate are those that can be appreciated by all music lovers. Ives's music can sensibly be approached from the context of the musical tradition he most admired: that of Bach, Beethoven, and Brahms. Those who love and revere the "three B's" can learn to love and revere Ives too, and for analogous reasons. His music has the capacity to enrich and enhance both our sensuous and our spiritual lives.

The work of most Ives specialists would currently suggest that a rather different, and much more arcane, orientation—or set of orientations—is necessary to establish an appropriate context for understanding Ives. The innocent music lover could easily come to assume that without an extensive knowledge of the many musical quotations employed by Ives in much of his work, and without a good deal of insight into matters of influence and chronology detailing the nature and extent of Ives's familiarity with the work of his contemporaries in Europe, there would be no hope of under-standing what is really significant in the music of this composer. Personally, I would hate to see befall Ives the fate that already seems sealed for his close contemporary, Arnold Schoenberg: the fate of having his musical oeuvre surrounded by voluminous scholarly work, of an aspect so forbid-ding to the typical music lover that it, in effect, closes off to a small elite the music it is supposedly seeking to open to wider understanding and investigation. (Perhaps someday an enterprising music scholar will give us "Schoenberg without tears," and make the convincing case that needs to be made for Schoenberg as an artist of potentially universal appeal and importance, a composer whose work typical music lovers can learn to appreciate and even love without studying the details of tone rows and serial theory.) In Schoenberg's case at least, one can trace many of the concerns in the specialized literature to sources in the work and words of the man himself. However, I suspect Ives would have been confused and disappointed by much that has been written about him to date—that he would have found it concerned too much with the "manner" and circum-stances of his musical output, rather than with its "substance."

So I must ask specialists to sympathize with a seeming paradox under-lying this book. By dealing with Ives in a general way here, which may seem to bypass many issues under intense scrutiny in the scholarly liter-ature, I am really arguing in the long run for the broader relevance and interest of that scholarly literature. In other words, specialized work on

Ives will seem that much more justifiable, and its discoveries that much more potentially important, to the extent that Ives is perceived as an artist of truly wide-ranging importance, whose appeal is not limited to specialists. I don't feel that an argument for this perception of Ives has yet been made as effectively as it could, and the desire to rectify this situation has probably been my strongest single motivation in undertaking this book. To make the argument convincingly, I obviously must give much of the current Ives scholarship a wide berth, and direct attention instead to the most basic issues, issues of self-evident import to all music lovers (including scholars).

If Ives is to be approached then from the context within which most listeners approach Mozart, Schubert, or Bartók, he will still initially seem a most unconventional composer—but not primarily because of matters upon which most of the current Ives literature is focused. The most striking peculiarity involves Ives's approach to *style*. Therefore, my second essential conviction is that Ives's style must be the core issue addressed by any basic study of his music. Ives's employment of musical style is at once his most idiosyncratic characteristic as a composer, and the most obvious initial stumbling block his music presents to the listener seeking appreciation and understanding. But Ives's approach to style is also, paradoxically and wonderfully, the key to unlocking what his music is most essentially *about*.

In a typical Ives work, the listener will find elements of modernism, of course. Many listeners still find twentieth-century musical modernism to be problematic in certain respects; however, this is not the source of the real stylistic difficulty in Ives. It is rather the *heterogeneity* of style within single works—the fact that modernistic passages can give way without warning to traditional-sounding music, or vice versa, or that strikingly different styles can even occur simultaneously—that truly sets Ives apart from the mainstream experience of most listeners.

The scholarly and critical literature has been, for the most part, disappointingly offhand or silent concerning this issue of style in the work of Ives. It will not do merely to assume that stylistic differences were of no importance to Ives, or that he simply used whatever material happened to be at hand to serve his purposes. Neither will a reliance on programmatic considerations, or on the identification of musical quotations, serve to explain away Ives's stylistic heterogeneity. This most prominent feature of his music must be faced squarely, and must be faced from the standpoint of *musical* communication.

We should at least entertain the hypothesis that the composer knew how stylistically "different" his music would sound to listeners of all backgrounds and experience (since the stylistic effect would have been, if anything, even more pronounced for the listeners of Ives's own time)—that he wanted this effect to be prominent, and to communicate ideas that were very important to him. This study is designed to reveal how deeply and thoroughly into Ives's aesthetic thought an investigation centered upon style can penetrate.

The third, and last, basic conviction underlying my study is that Ives's music is best introduced chiefly through the medium of his songs. There are a number of reasons I can offer for this. Most obviously, songs are ideal for analytical purposes. They are short enough to allow consideration of a significant number of works both in detail and as totalities. The clarity of texture in the song medium facilitates ready understanding on the part of both specialists and non-specialists, and the presence of words provides a graceful and accessible source of reference points in a score.

In the specific case of Ives, the songs are ideally suited to support a thorough study of the composer's employment of style. Ives's songs are numerous and diverse enough to offer a comprehensive overview of his compositional world. Traditionally styled and traditionally unified songs certainly exist in the Ives corpus, but so do many songs that represent Ives at his most "difficult" and idiosyncratic. In this respect, as in many others, Ives's songs mirror his diverse output in other genres as well as his output as a whole. A careful look at several well-chosen songs can certainly give as effective an introduction to this composer's techniques as the study of any one of his famous large-scale instrumental compositions. Works other than songs will also receive occasional attention in this study, in order to demonstrate directly the relevance of a stylistic examination of Ives's songs to issues raised by his oeuvre as a whole.

And Ives's songs are easy to love. I have frequently encountered professional musicians, as well as other music lovers, who have substantial difficulties with Ives, but who readily admit to admiring and enjoying the songs. There is, I suspect, an obvious and very good reason why Ives's songs are so widely admired. Although Ives made important contributions to many genres, there are other equally excellent American composers of symphonic, choral, and chamber music. However, there is no writer of songs in English in the twentieth century—and I'm tempted to say in any period—whose output manifests the scope and diversity, imagination and daring, and at last, the sheer mastery revealed by that of Ives. There is no kind of song Ives couldn't write, whether religious, sentimental, humorous, philosophical, political, traditional, or radical. In fact, and this was his most extraordinary contribution, many of his finest and most individual songs incorporate several of these characteristics simultaneously.

A great many of Ives's songs are set to his own wonderful words, words rich with import for anyone wishing to understand the composer's philosophical outlook and deepest feelings. In this study, Ives's words will be allowed to speak for themselves, and will not be viewed as an "explanation" for the musical aspects of Ives's work. The danger in working with songs is that of falling into a programmatic type of analysis, which can limit the relevance of the approach to one particular song at one particular time, can compromise the potential of the approach for any application outside of the song repertoire, and can have the unfortunate but unavoidable tendency to devalue the essentially musical procedures being utilized by the composer.

I have strived throughout this study to use Ives's songs as a means of addressing his *musical* thought processes. These processes may be enriched and supplemented extensively by the words to his songs, but they are in no way justified by those words. In any fine song, musical technique and coherence must "speak" for themselves. Otherwise, the accompanying words are compromised, along with every other aspect of the aesthetic experience.

I hope the reader will not find it surprising that, in seeking a form for my work, I have followed an example suggested in many works by Ives. Rather than introducing ideas individually and in their simplest forms, and then developing them in a traditionally logical fashion, Ives often chooses to commence by thrusting us into the immediacy of an already developed, complex experience. Then he will allow aspects of that complexity and richness to "spin off," to reveal themselves as separable elements, and have their independent ramifications pursued. Sometimes the simplest statements of ideas are reserved for the endings of works; at other times, works return at their conclusions to the complexities exposed at their outsets.

The main body of my book begins with musings on the complexity of Ives's approach to style. The first piece to be explored thoroughly is the song "Ann Street," and although it is a rather short work, it is no sense a simple one; it exposes the reader immediately to a full-blown example of Ives's compositional maturity, demonstrating the challenge and excitement of his stylistic "difficulty" and intricacy. The discussion of "Ann Street" raises many issues and suggests various modes of thinking about Ives's work, several of which are allowed to "spin off" into other discussions of related and tangential issues and pieces. These, in turn, suggest further developments and digressions. Highly specific commentary on individual works is alternated with general aesthetic observations and questioning, in what is intended to mimic a kind of Ivesian dialectic of styles and approaches to music.

1

Style and Substance

I know I'm listening to Ives when there's something "wrong."
—*George Perle, to his class on twentieth-century music*

Dear Mr. Price: Please don't try to make things nice! All the wrong notes are right.
—*Charles Ives, to his copyist*

George Perle, the distinguished composer and theorist, was not intending to cast aspersions on Ives's music (some of which he admires) when he referred to something sounding "wrong" about it. He was simply trying to express an important critical observation in language that the non-musicians as well as the musicians in his course would readily understand. Ives was dealing with the same issue of seemingly "wrong" notes and apparent stylistic anomalies in his music when he scrawled the humorous note to his copyist on the manuscript of "The Fourth of July," a movement from his symphony *New England Holidays.* Ives's music does not behave like that of his predecessors and contemporaries in the Western art music tradition, and if we come to it expecting it to behave like that other music, we will react with confusion, at least.

Consider the opening to Ives's famous piece, *The Unanswered Question.*

After about a minute of extremely slow, flowing, consonant, hymn-like music for strings, a solo trumpet enters with a totally disjunct, non-tonal phrase that sounds (and—this is the point—is *calculated* to sound) as if it came from another piece, if not another planet, entirely.

To cite what is perhaps an even more extreme example, consider the excerpt from the "Hawthorne" movement of Ives's "Concord" Sonata shown in Ex. 1–1. To anyone, musician or non-musician, who is familiar with the appearance of a traditional piano score, this music even *looks* crazy. It is no wonder that the majority of those who encountered this first published score by Ives in the 1920s and 1930s treated it as some kind of joke, as have many others up to the present day who have not cared to investigate seriously. What is that poor little chordal fragment in 6/8 meter (marked "very slowly" and to be played very softly) doing sandwiched between passages of very loud, very fast, unmetered music of a totally different texture, melodic style, and harmonic language? The superficial evidence suggests a composer who didn't know or, worse, didn't even care what he was doing.

During his lifetime, Ives was accused of being such a composer, and the charges have been repeated up to the present day, both by some who are

EXAMPLE 1–1. Ives, Piano Sonata No. 2 ("Concord, Mass., 1840–1860"), second ("Hawthorne") movement, excerpt.

legitimately confused and by some who should know better. As an example of the latter, I digress briefly to offer a personal reminiscence.

Several years ago a composer acquaintance of mine came to dinner. In the course of a brief discussion about Ives, he offered as a criticism of the "Concord" Sonata his opinion that one could shuffle the pages of that work into any order and still come out with something no more or less coherent than what one had originally. An hour or two later, this composer asked us to listen to him play his latest composition. It was a piano work consisting of fifty-two parts of varying length, identified by the names of playing cards ("two of hearts," "Jack of spades," and so forth). The ordering of the parts for any given performance was determined arbitrarily by shuffling a deck of cards beforehand, and arranging the pages of the work accordingly. There was clearly no connection in the composer's mind between his criticism of the "Concord" Sonata and the form of his own piece. This irony is independent of the further irony that most serious students of the "Concord" Sonata would disagree strongly with his assessment of it.

At the heart of Ives's strangeness and originality is his attitude toward style. "Style" is inevitably a tricky term to use, since it has so many connotations and applications. I will be using the term here to imply the *range of expectation* that operates within the musical language of a piece. The range of expectation in an Ives work is qualitatively and quantitatively different from that in the music of his predecessors and contemporaries.

Upon hearing just the first few measures of a Mozart piece, we have a pretty accurate idea, without needing to formulate it consciously, what the musical language of the piece is, and what kinds of musical events are likely to follow that opening. The more Mozart we hear, the more clearly we perceive the language through which the composer expresses himself, the more easily we grasp what is and isn't likely to happen in a particular Mozart piece, and the more we develop a sense of Mozart's *style*. Although the musical language involved is radically different, the same statements may also be made about Schoenberg. However, when we hear the beginning of an Ives piece, we *don't* necessarily know what kinds of things will and will not follow. And the more Ives we hear, the *less* comfortable we may feel making predictions.

In a way, our ability to sense the style of a work establishes a kind of frame around it, defining a deliberately limited sphere of activity within which the work operates. The great advantage of this "limitation" is, obviously, that it facilitates the establishment and maintenance of a shared, if unspoken, common ground between creator and audience, a mutually understood context within which communication may take place with some ease and fluency. The stylistic "frame" locates and confines the work within a specific area of conceptual space. The more familiar the style utilized, the more easily the basis of communication is established. As creators refine and perfect their individual styles, they increase the subtleties of language and expression available within the chosen frames. In the case of Bach or Mozart, the individual style may achieve such depth and richness that, to a receptive listener, it seems to belie the existence of any "limiting" frame at all; paradoxically, it may well be true that the intangible frame is the greatest source of liberation, rather than confinement, for many great creators.

Ives often uses styles for a traditional purpose—that is, to establish a frame of reference. This is especially true when he is using, or evoking, more traditional and familiar styles. But he uses the implied frame around his styles for an additional purpose as well, since he discovered that the existence of the frame could make possible the unfamiliar, but valuable, artistic effect achieved by deliberately breaking the frame. This happens when styles shift abruptly within an Ives piece, and an entirely new range of aesthetic possibilities is opened for creative exploration. When this takes place, we can no longer speak of the music as being composed *in* a particular style. Rather, the music is composed *with styles;* the whole issue of style becomes part of the music's subject matter, on a very profound level. In many ways, Ives's work is *about* style, which is why an analytical approach to Ives that centers around stylistic questions can go right to the heart of this composer's aesthetics, individuality, and importance.

Ives's stylistic heterogeneity presses the issue of new approaches to musical thought, and musical thought-process, much more forcibly than the presentation of new approaches to pitch, rhythm, and texture ever could by themselves—although such novelties are also always occurring in his music. This is true because the expectation of stylistic unity or predictability—at least on some level—is, I believe, more deeply rooted in our traditional experiences of art than any particular grammatical system. Ives shatters this expectation in order to create challenging and unprecedented expressive and formal experiences out of the compositional manipulation of stylistic change.

Breaking the stylistic frame has many dangers, of course. That it can easily cause consternation for the listener accustomed to stylistic homogeneity is an obvious danger, one illustrated profusely by the critical reception accorded much of Ives's music. The danger of real formal chaos is another. How Ives attempted to create some sense of order without maintaining a single stylistic frame in his music will be the subject of the discussion that is to follow.

Ives's use of stylistic heterogeneity in his music differs markedly from the phenomenon of what I might call "substyles," which can be found in the work of many composers. Substyles form individual, separable aspects of what is, ultimately, a unified musical language the composer seeks to make his own. In Bach or in Mozart, for example, various "national" substyles (Italian, French, German, or English) are subsumed within a larger framework of personal style that embraces elements of variety but also imposes unity. We can recognize the composer's stylistic *voice,* even when he alters his accent. In individual works, and over the span of their entire careers, one can speak meaningfully of Bach's and Mozart's respective styles, even as each composer's style expands, narrows, and evolves from work to work and throughout his creative lifetime.

I don't think I can speak in the same way of Ives's music having substyles, because I can't articulate to what the purported substyles in his work are subordinate. Perhaps a finer scholar than I will one day be able to spell out organizing, inclusive grammatical principles that govern *all* of Ives's melodic, harmonic, rhythmic, and textural styles. I suspect, however, that such general principles, could they be articulated, might prove so general as to be meaningless in defining a *style* as we commonly conceive of it, precisely because the range of expectation allowed by these principles would be much too broad.

In the familiar music of most other composers, the point of stylistic changes and variations—of substyles—is to provide variety and contrast. Ultimately, however, these substyles also provide a potent source of artistic unity by demonstrating their congruence within a larger, embracing, but traditionally unified conception of a single musical language. Divergence, as an artistic tool, is finally subservient to convergence. The moments of violent disruption in the music of Beethoven, for example, serve in the end to demonstrate the power of his unifying control over the most apparently dichotomous elements within his stylistic repertoire. Seeming disharmony is revealed paradoxically as an aspect of a larger, truer harmony.

In Ives, on the other hand, the point of stylistic divergence is: stylistic divergence. In his music, I don't think he intends for us to experience the sense of one larger, dominating style that enfolds and contains various substyles. I think Ives wants to bring us face to face with the realization that *no* such unifying style may exist—to force us to confront the diversity as such, and to deal with it on its own terms. The controlling question is not how this music demonstrates overall, unifying stylistic principles, but rather, can it demonstrate new, convincing principles of structure that do not depend on style in the traditional way as a unifying device? Or, to put the question in other ways: Can there be a means of intelligible artistic discourse that does not ultimately minimize or downplay stylistic divergence but instead *emphasizes* stylistic disruptions as the most salient, necessary facts of (musical) life? Can one make art that accepts heterogeneity simply as itself without turning it into a larger homogeneity; art that makes the phenomenon of incongruence ultimately subordinate to nothing? Can there be art which makes stylistic divergence its subject matter—and, even more than that, its message and meaning?

10

In Mozart's *A Musical Joke* (*Ein musikalischer Spass*, K. 522), outrageous "wrong notes" and other stylistic infelicities on various levels of subtlety are utilized by the composer to parody incompetent composers and performers. Stylistic incongruities like the intrusion of a whole-tone scale into the end of an already overextended violin cadenza obviously function here as "jokes" (Ex. 1–2). Clearly the breaking of the stylistic frame cannot be considered seriously as an artistic device in the context of Mozart's musical language. On the other hand, when the consonant hymn-like music of the strings in Ives's *The Unanswered Question* is interrupted by the outrageously "wrong notes" of the trumpet, it is indeed occasion for "a contemplation of a serious matter" (as Ives himself described it). Ives demands that we consider the breaking of the frame soberly; what in Mozart disrupts the discourse of a piece for Ives *becomes* the discourse of a piece.

It might well be asked how Ives differs from close contemporaries of his—such as Mahler, Stravinsky, and Copland—who also experimented with aspects of style. Mahler stretched stylistic divergence about as far as it could possibly go while still remaining within the orbit of what we call late Romantic style. There are significant kinships between Ives and Mahler, but Ives steps over a line that Mahler never actually crosses. Stravinsky definitely does deal with stylistic heterogeneity over the span of his career, but the stylistic changes occur from work to work rather than within individual works. This is very important because Stravinsky's music, therefore, does not challenge the unwritten law that any *particular* artwork needs to be stylistically unified. These observations about Stravinsky hold equally true for Copland, who explored stylistic heterogeneity during his career in much the same fashion as Stravinsky.

It seems safe to assert that during the period when Ives was composing the major works that constitute his challenge to the accepted conventions of musical style, there was nobody else in the Western musical tradition working intensively and systematically along these same lines. Among his contemporaries, the real parallels to Ives are in literature. One may find clear analogies to Ives's way of working with style in such celebrated works of literary modernism as T. S. Eliot's *The Waste Land*, with its provocative mixture of languages, quotations, and poetic styles, and James Joyce's *Ulysses*, with its intricate overall structure based on juxtapositions of varying literary styles and techniques. If Ives's basic artistic medium had been literature, he might well have been regarded as part of a modernist mainstream, rather than as an isolated, unique, and problematic figure. (Ives, however, was certainly unfamiliar with writers like Eliot or Joyce when he was writing his music.)

Ives's very real engagement with the most serious aesthetic issues of style and coherence is evident throughout the pages of his own book, *Essays Before A Sonata*. There, one finds a dense, grammatically challenging

11

EXAMPLE 1–2. Mozart, *A Musical Joke*, third movement, violin cadenza (mm. 63–77).

prose that mixes linear reasoning with digression, seriousness with humor, and original ideas with quotations in a fashion that creates the literary equivalent of Ives's most complex music. And in this prose, Ives makes it clear that he is supremely aware of what issues he is raising in his music and why he is raising them:

> Orderly reason does not always have to be a visible part of all great things. . . . Initial coherence to-day may be dullness to-morrow probably because formal or outward unity depends so much on repetition, sequences, antitheses, paragraphs with inductions and summaries.

Certainly not all of Ives's music raises or deals with these issues. One might be convinced that stylistic *change*, at least, is inevitable within the context of any of Ives's later big works, until one experiences the third movement of his Fourth Symphony—one of the composer's last, and most ambitious, major works. Here, he presents the listener with an eight-minute fugal movement in a traditional and quite consistent style from beginning to end! Ives's utilization of stylistic heterogeneity is neither consistent nor consistently antithetical to some general, traditional procedures of creating formal unity. Nevertheless, the majority of his most characteristic and important works do focus on these kinds of stylistic issues in very direct and provocative ways.

During the last three decades, a poly-stylistic approach has become common in many of the contemporary arts. One might wonder whether this development has posthumously "vindicated" Ives, and assured his latter-day acceptance as an anticipator of the new "mainstream." But even within a musical landscape that includes Elliott Carter, George Crumb, George Rochberg, Peter Maxwell Davies, Luciano Berio, and Karlheinz Stockhausen, Ives's work is still often seen as isolated and problematic.

Elliott Carter, a composer famous for stylistic experimentation in his own work, has been aware of, and interested in, Ives throughout his own creative life. Carter has written that he has "always been fascinated by the polyrhythmic aspect of Ives's music, as well as its multiple layering, but perplexed at times by the disturbing lack of musical and stylistic continuity." If one listens to Carter's music, these words will not seem surprising. Despite the different "characters" assigned to specific instruments in a work like his second String Quartet, or the obvious dichotomies between the instrumental protagonists in a work like the Double Concerto for Piano and Harpsichord, Carter ultimately emerges as a composer who works with substyles, as I have defined them, not with styles in the Ivesian sense. Indeed, implicit in Carter's statement quoted above is a firmly held concept of "stylistic continuity" as a fixed desideratum for quality and coherence in an art form. For all the obvious modernity of Carter's musical language, his aesthetic stance remains, in many ways, relatively traditional.

The case is different to some degree with composers like George Crumb and George Rochberg. Their work during the last twenty years or so reveals some obvious surface kinships with that of Ives, as well as some common aesthetic concerns. Yet Crumb's uses of stylistically surprising quotations and Rochberg's carefully patterned alternations of style seem extremely cautious if compared to analogous passages in Ives's work. Had Ives lived to hear their music, I suspect he might have criticized it as being excessively well-mannered.

There is sometimes a rough, effusive, and *messy* quality to Ives, a quality one never senses in the work of more artistically self-conscious composers like Crumb, Rochberg, Carter, Berio, or Stockhausen. All these other men are products of a historically-oriented culture of art, artists, and artistic behavior, and are very much aware of their places within that culture. Ives might have voiced this as a criticism of their limitations. I intend no such thing, wishing only to point out that these creators are, by training and personal election, part of a tradition from which Ives to some degree, and very intentionally, distanced himself, even as he maintained and utilized selected aspects of that tradition in his own work. It is no wonder that, up to the present day, professional musicians in large numbers retain a significant suspicion of Ives and of what he was doing. It is also no surprise that members of the listening public accustomed to music-making within the tradition from which Ives distanced himself should continue to find his music peculiar, even if they are familiar and comfortable with recent music that might seem in superficial ways to bear his influence or to share elements in common with his.

The "messiness" of some of Ives's work has doubtless been a major source of consternation to many listeners, and a major cause of criticism for alleged carelessness or even outright incompetence from many commentators, including other composers. The "messiness" most frequently arises from Ives's very intentional evocation of the flavor and spirit of amateur music-making, on the one hand, and from his willingness to risk *apparent* chaos in the interests of inclusiveness on the other. These complex matters will be discussed later. For the moment, it is important simply to stress that the "messiness" in Ives's music is frequently deliberate, and often highly calculated, on his part. It plays an important role in delineating his special perspective on the traditional culture of professional composition and music-making. In a way, it is both the result and the cause of that perspective.

Elliott Carter asserts that the "lack of musical and stylistic continuity" that he finds perplexing in Ives is "caused largely by the constant use of musical quotations in many works." Certainly the matter of quotations in Ives's music is complicated and problematic, and contributes significantly to the "difficulty" of his music. How should the listener understand Ives's employment of quotations and evaluate their stylistic effect and importance?

There is no question that Ives had profound personal associations with most of the symphonic, religious, and popular music he quoted in his works. However, to assume or assert, as so many do, that it is necessary for listeners to share—or to learn to share—these associations in order to understand the *artistic* import of Ives's use of quotations is to take a curiously literal and unimaginative approach to the matter. Such an approach seems particularly inappropriate in light of the fact that Ives's employment of quotations is most frequently non-literal and, almost always, highly imaginative. (For an illustration of this, see the discussion in Chapter 6 of "General William Booth Enters Into Heaven," and Examples 6–5 and 6–6.)

Ives lived a very private life as a composer and his compositions may well have functioned, in some ways, as a kind of personal diary for him. However, the key to his importance as a creative artist lies in the fact that he could articulate these musical confidences in a way that rendered their local and personal genesis inessential to an appreciation of them by outsiders, and ultimately unimportant in terms of the larger artistic truths they captured. In terms of the artistic form and meaning of his music, Ives's quotations, however they may have functioned for him personally, need not be viewed as quotations of specific works or songs, or even necessarily as evocations of specific kinds of occasions, time periods, or landscapes. They may be heard as quotations of *styles*. Their function is a formal one. They create meaning and stimulate emotion, not through dependence on personal association, but through their interaction with the other stylistic elements in a particular work, and through the formal and affective associations their styles create in the context of the surrounding music.

Of course, the more that is learned about any composer's background, the more the appreciation of details in his art is potentially enriched. Naturally, it can become a part of the meaningful experience of an Ives piece if one recognizes a hymn he is quoting, or at least recognizes that it is one. Sometimes, the unsung words of a quoted tune even form an interesting subtext in the music. But it is important not to get the priorities backwards, and the priorities in the case of Ives seem to have gotten tangled even more than in the cases of most artists. It is Ives's *music* that makes the details about its creator, creation, and cultural background interesting and important, and more than quaint curiosities.

That music stands ready, and is most qualified, to address the receptive listener on the basis of musical expression and communication alone. Ives may well be a "difficult" composer, but the stylistic and conceptual "difficulties" of his best work do not stem from an interest in complexity for its own sake. Rather, they stem from Ives's respect for the wide audience he reached toward in his work—a respect manifested in the form of a refusal to talk down to his listeners. It is worth making the effort to achieve an appreciation of Ives because the music offers such manifold and special rewards for the effort. The following pages, by exploring some of the basic ways in which Ives manipulates style, are addressed to his "ideal listener" in the hope of illuminating the feelings and meanings in his music, and thereby rendering this extraordinary music less difficult to understand.

Into Analysis

Substance in a human-art-quality suggests the body of a conviction which has its birth in the spiritual consciousness, whose youth is nourished in the moral consciousness, and whose maturity as a result of all this growth is then represented in a mental image. This is appreciated by the intuition, and somehow translated into expression by "manner"—a process always less important than it seems . . .

At any rate, we are going to be arbitrary enough to claim, with no definite qualification, that substance can be expressed in music, and that it is the only valuable thing in it . . . Substance has something to do with character. Manner has nothing to do with it. The "substance" of a tune comes from somewhere near the soul, and the "manner" comes from—God knows where.

—*Charles Ives, from the epilogue to* Essays Before a Sonata

Ives's remarks concerning substance and manner in music are the kinds of statements that get him into trouble in certain circles. Formulations about "spiritual consciousness" and "moral consciousness" are, to say the least, out of sight (if not out of mind), and definitely out of favor in contemporary scholarly and critical discourse—and have been for some time. In our highly "scientific," anti-Romantic, detail- and craft-conscious era of artistic history (and criticism), much of Ives's writing could be construed as lending support to those who would like to assume that, for this composer, intention is all that really should matter to a creator and to his audience, with traditional considerations of style, form, and technique—of *artistry,* even— counting for little or nothing at all.

But these statements by Ives also create a backlash of problems for those who would defend him against charges of carelessness or incompetence, or against the ironic charge of "amateurism." For if one chooses to demonstrate Ives's compositional craftsmanship through traditional techniques of analysis, which can be done in the case of many works, isn't one falling right into the trap of raising manner over substance? And if I invent a new method for dealing in some systematic way with Ives's use of musical styles, am I not also just calling attention to aspects of his manner and thereby diverting attention away from the very substance he most valued and would want me most to value?

Analyzing most of Ives's music is challenging. Analyzing it in a way that truly addresses the stylistic issues it presents is more challenging still. Analyzing it in a way that remains true to the spirit that created the music is most difficult of all. Yet couldn't similar or analogous statements be made about many of the creators and creations throughout history that we have come to value most? In the case of Ives, the nature of his mind and art operated in such a way as to make the issues, problems, and possible contradictions just that much more apparent and pointed. This remains as true today as when he was actually composing his music. In this sense, as in so many others, he is a truly *contemporary* composer. One could even claim with some legitimacy that Ives composed as he did in order to direct attention to questions of manner and substance in the most forceful way possible.

My conviction is that when Ives's stylistic manner is analyzed in a fashion true to his substance, then the distinction between the two ultimately collapses. This is true chiefly because Ives's employment of style is so challenging that it virtually obligates the analyst to search for its motivating "meaning" and underlying principles of organization. In Ives's finest music, there is no breach between its external form and its inner content; as in so much of the greatest art, the same controlling impulses appear to govern both the whole and the character and arrangement of its individual parts. Ives's often peculiar manner is thus in fact *necessary* to the appropriate expression of his substance. In his best work, he succeeds in rendering distinctions between the two obsolete, so that when we properly study his manner we are in fact studying his substance. The analyses that follow are designed to illustrate and defend this conviction.

2

Juxtaposition and Sequence (I): A Walk on "Ann Street"

Let us begin the discussion of style, form, and content in the music of Ives with the extremely short song, "Ann Street." It's a late piece, written in 1921, fully representative of the composer's mature work, and is ideal for the purposes of this study. Its brevity facilitates familiarity and discussion; the complete score, all two pages of it, appears as Ex. 2–1. Within its brief duration, "Ann Street" contains as many, if not more, stylistic shifts as other typical Ives pieces that are several times as long.

Ives, an insurance man by profession, knew the New York business district and its Ann Streets very well. He must have appreciated how successfully Maurice Morris's newspaper poem captured the breathless pace and feeling of impersonality that characterizes this particular corner of Manhattan. In Ives's setting, "Ann Street" speeds by with enough diverse material in it to inspire five or six songs by other composers—but then, that's life in the Big Apple. Gunther Schuller, who completed an instrumental arrangement of what he called this "utterly remarkable" song, speaks of the "rapidity and yet complete naturalness with which the piece

EXAMPLE 2–1. Ives, "Ann Street," complete.

From: Thirty Four Songs.
Copyright © 1933 Merion Music, Inc.
Used By Permission Of The Publisher

(*continued*)

changes mood, character, tempo, and meter every three or four bars."
These surface changes divide the little song into a relatively large number
of clearly perceived "sections," which are listed in Table 2–1.

To understand what happens in the music to create these numerous
sectional divisions, we can direct our attention to many different aspects

TABLE 2–1

"Ann Street": Sectional Divisions Created by Changes in Musical Style

Section	Text	Measure Numbers
1	(Piano introduction)	1–3
2	Quaint name—Ann street. width of same,—ten feet.	4–7
3	Barnums mob—Ann street, far from obsolete.	8–9
4	(Piano interlude) Narrow, yes, Ann street,	10–11
5	But business,	11 (last notes)
6	Both feet.	12
7	(Piano interlude: Nassau crosses Ann St.)	13–15
8	Sun just hits Ann street, then it quits—Some greet!	16–19
9	Rather short, Ann street . . .	20

of style. The rapid, rhythmically emphatic, loud, and chromatic music of the song's piano introduction (Section 1) contrasts in almost every way with the softer, slower, gentle, duple-metered diatonic music that characterizes Section 2. With the onset of Section 3, melodic style, harmonic language, rhythmic organization, tempo, dynamic level, and the use of keyboard register all change again. Although the idiom is now highly chromatic, and the music faster and louder than in Section 2, I'm not sure it would be correct to describe this as a return to the style of the piano introduction, especially since the rhythmic character of Section 3 differs so markedly from anything heard before in the piece. (Notice especially the arrangement of the piano part here in groups of seven eighth-notes and the complex rhythmic counterpoint this creates with the voice part, which is apparently striving to carry over from Section 2 some feeling of a syncopated $\frac{2}{4}$ meter.) Section 4 continues and intensifies the chromaticism of Section 3, but the sudden absence of the piano's lower register, and of the B-flat major triad heard so prominently in that register in Section 3, places us abruptly at this point in a new, utterly non-triadic ("atonal?") style that also differs rhythmically from the music of the harmonically ambiguous, but triadically oriented, style we had just been hearing.

A description of "Ann Street" along these lines could easily be continued up to the end of the piece. Clearly Ives's stylistic changes involve multiple musical factors, so that regardless of whether one is predisposed to define

23

style harmonically, rhythmically, texturally, or through a combination of elements, one can hear the sectional divisions that are enumerated in the preceding chart. The only two adjacent sections that might seem very close in style are Sections 8 and 9. However, Section 8 has essentially a whole-tone flavor, while Section 9 is almost exclusively diatonic—except for a lone C♯ neighbor-note to D in the vocal line, the music of this final section is confined to the tones of a B-flat major scale.

Despite the stylistic changes, it is also true that there are similarities and connections among the sections of this song. These certainly play at least a background role in providing some degree of overall coherence and traditional continuity. One might ask how far traditional analytical approaches, which do not deal directly with stylistic divergence, could take us toward an understanding of the connective tissue in "Ann Street." The answer is: surprisingly far, so long as one ignores the foreground issue of stylistic change. In fact, the piece can be shown to be so obviously coherent from certain traditional points of view that one must wonder why Ives chose to make it *sound*, from a conventional standpoint, so *in*coherent. And thus we arrive at an unfortunately common analytical conundrum. If we ignore what we want most to know about this piece—the most obvious and compelling questions of compositional and expressive intent and meaning—then traditional analysis can tell us a lot about it. (Or, to return to Ives's terminology, if we ignore the song's substance, we can use traditional analysis to discover much about the song's manner!)

One standard line of analytical attack here would be to look at the intervallic content of both linear (melodic) and vertical (harmonic) structures in the piece. Without being either comprehensive or systematic, I can easily sketch the broad outlines of this approach as applied to "Ann Street," and indicate the kinds of things it will reveal. One obvious place to start would be with the vocal line itself, in order to see how Ives constructs a melody *in toto*.

The voice part of "Ann Street" is logically, and tightly, structured around the development of a single motive, proclaimed right at the outset on "Quaint name—Ann street," and consisting of a descending perfect fourth (A to E) subdivided into a major second and a minor third. The descending direction of this motive, and its constituent intervals of second and third, provide the basis for the ensuing events in the melody. For example, the phrase on "Barnums mob—Ann street" is a descending gesture structured around the fourth D–A and the interval G♯–F, which is actually a minor third. The fourth here is subdivided into a *minor* second and a *major* third (D–D♭–A), creating a variant of the opening motive. It is even possible to see in the concluding three pitches of this phrase, G♯–G♮–F, a compression of the opening motive into smaller intervals.

Successive developments in the melodic line can be perceived in similar

24

terms, and together create a convincing overall form. The melody continues to utilize smaller and smaller intervals until it reaches its midpoint on "But business," where, instead of continuing a chromatic scale downward, it turns a repeated E into an inspired octave leap and inaugurates a process of interval expansion. Major thirds and major seconds provide the inter-vallic material right through "Some greet!"; the end product of expansion is found in the final phrase of the song, a decorated variant of the opening motive that now spans a *fifth* instead of a fourth. The same kind of intervallic consistency can be demonstrated within the piano accompaniment, and it exists as well between voice and piano.

Another traditional approach to the analysis of early twentieth-century music would focus on the question of pitch organization—here not in terms of intervals alone, but in reference to the possible presence in the piece of pitch "centers," which function in some sense analogously to the keys of traditional tonal music. From our survey of the voice line for intervallic content, the prominence of the pitch A in the vocal part, virtually through-out the piece, may already be obvious. Even before the singer's entrance, the importance of A is forcefully asserted by the piano, which opens the piece with a long, lone, fortissimo A, held as a low pedal point right through the end of Section 1.

As the song progresses, the pitch A establishes clear relationships with certain other pitches: in Section 2, with the G and E below it in the voice, and with the D and C above it in the piano. This same D is important immediately afterwards in the vocal line as the starting note of the phrase "Barnums mob—Ann street"; the phrase which follows, "far from obso-lete," ends on E, and A is precisely in the middle of this span of notes. The A is also exactly in the center of the chromatic segment that presents the next vocal phrase, "Narrow, yes, Ann street!" It is not difficult to see, even without detailed or systematic analysis, that these and similar rela-tionships carry through the piece in various ways. (Furthermore, the rel-ative prominence—or lack of prominence—of the focal A at any given point, along with the particular relationships other pitch elements establish with the A at that point, play their part in the delineation of stylistic sections within the song.) The abruptness of the song's ending, its sense of incom-pleteness, has a great deal to do, of course, with the cessation of the voice line, on G, without the anticipated return to A. The piano adds to the "open" ending in Section 9 by presenting A only as a relatively subordinate pitch within its gently rocking repeated figures, and by substituting a very prominent E♭ for the previously important E.

This is all very well and good. "Ann Street" is clearly a well–crafted piece. But "Ann Street" is *not* clearly a unified and coherent piece in the traditional sense. To call this song a *traditionally* unified and coherent piece is to deliberately overlook, or thoroughly subordinate, the most distinctive aspect of its musical character and what we notice most prominently as listeners: those marked and frequent changes of style. Failing to address these stylistic changes is, in effect, operating in a manner that opposes the aesthetic substance of the music. Traditional analysis would seek to find unity and coherence despite the variegated surface of "Ann Street."

I think it is possible to proceed otherwise, and to find some new sources of artistic meaning and organization on that variegated surface. In fact, the stylistic changes in "Ann Street" create an overall design, and thus may be seen as producing unity and coherence—on a large scale—rather than confusion. It seems reasonably obvious that, if we regard Section 1 as an introduction presenting various elements which are explored methodically in the body of the song, then Sections 2 through 9 present a stylistic arch in which distinct units of increasing complexity, rhythmic activity, chromaticism, and dissonance are followed by units that return to more consonant, diatonic, and rhythmically placid music.

The two springers of this stylistic arch are Sections 2 and 9, not merely because of their structural positions but, most significantly, because they share the most closely related styles of any two sections of the piece. These sections come closer to pure diatonicism than any other parts of the song. Section 2 confines itself to the tones of a major scale built on F, with the single exception of the high F♯ in its final measure (which could be an anticipation of this identical F♯ in Section 3, where it is heard three times; a possible small-scaled instance of the kind of stylistic overlapping that is of great significance in other works of Ives). Section 9 uses the tones of a B-flat major scale with, again, a lone deviation in the form of the C♯ neighbor-note to D in the vocal line. Furthermore, one may remark the syncopated reiteration of an A-minor triad in the inner lines of the piano part in Section 2, and the analogous prominence of the G-minor triad in the piano part of Section 9.

Sections 3 and 8 play complementary roles in the stylistic arch of "Ann Street." Although they do not share even approximately identical styles, they each utilize both diatonic and non-diatonic elements, and are consequently ideally suited for their positions in the pattern. Section 3 moves the piece away from the style of Section 2 toward greater complexity, while Section 8, moving away from the complexity, heralds and makes aurally logical a return to stylistic simplicity.

The middle portion of the arch consists of Sections 4 through 7, with Section 5 as the keystone. This middle area of stylistic complexity begins and ends with music for piano alone; the two piano interludes create two additional points of structural symmetry in the arch. The vocal octave and big piano chord of Section 5 proclaim the stylistic midpoint in an emphatic way, while isolating and underlining what is probably the central idea of the entire poem (and of real life on the real Ann Street): *"Business"*! The reassertion in Section 5 of the important pitches A and E in a relatively less dissonant, more diatonic-sounding context (even if Ives's chord does suggest a confusion between A major and A minor) is obviously significant and logical from a stylistic point of view; at the height of complexity, the reassertion recalls for us where we have been and launches us toward the downward arc.

In "Ann Street," and in much of Ives's music, the alterations of musical style—while appearing to disrupt or even destroy continuity, form, and unity as traditionally conceived—actually *create* continuity, form, and unity on another level of perception. A multi-leveled view of the musical work is one that is not only encouraged, but actually demanded, by Ives's procedures if we are to make sense of them. Such a view yields important insights and can frequently reveal fascinating richness and ambiguities built into the work in a way that suggests complexities of perspective in the visual arts. An obvious but significant analogy would be to the cubist canvasses of Picasso and Braque, where traditional "realistic" perspective is completely disrupted in the interest of creating a new kind of painterly coherence on the two-dimensional surface. Like a cubist painting, "Ann Street" offers simultaneous varying perspectives on its subject, perspectives that together create a radically new kind of artistic unity.

Perhaps the most striking example of multiple perspective in "Ann Street" is the way in which its ending appears to be "closed" and "open" at the same time. There is a sense of formal completion achieved because of the character and position of Section 9 in the song's stylistic arch, but this comes without significant direct repetition of earlier material or any ultimate resolution or closure of the pitch relationships suggested during the course of the piece. Both the expressive and philosophical implications of this are striking; the compositional potential suggested by the treatment of style in this tiny song is impressive indeed. (Again, one may profitably think of the analogy to cubism.) Surely this is artistic *substance*.

Ives's "mental image" of substance, conveyed through the unique manner of "Ann Street," is one of existence as a multi-faceted, variegated challenge posed by a succession of rapidly progressing experiences. While appearing on the surface to be disjointed, these experiences do reveal certain kinds of large-scale ordering, or patterns, when viewed from a different perspective. However, the orderings and patterns that may be discovered in existence are, of necessity, tentative, unfinished, and "imperfect," due to the nature of existence as *process*, rather than as product. The significance of the song's ending (one does not want to call it a conclusion) can perhaps be stated this way: After a succession of varied experiences, one may return toward one's point of departure, but that point can never really be reached again, since one's perception has been irrevocably altered by the intervening events.

In "Ann Street," style and substance are clearly inseparable, because the constantly changing style is not simply a vehicle for the presentation of ideas, but is itself the embodiment of profound and novel ideas about the character not only of musical experience, but of experience itself. To accept the stylistic arch, and its role in the creation of form, is not only to accept the validity of a new and broader usage of style and form in musical expression, but also to accept, by implication, a world (a universe?) of change, inconsistency, diversity, and non-recurrence (at least, non-*literal* recurrence). This clearly is Ives's view of the world, and he just as clearly views the artist's function in this world as one of suggesting patterns of understanding *without* resorting to the usual kinds of simplifying, homogenizing, and repetition that have traditionally been seen as necessary to the creation of "fine," "professional," and "accomplished" art.

The text of "Ann Street" has been downplayed deliberately in the discussion so far in order to focus as directly as possible on considerations of musical style and substance—considerations that can readily be applied to much of Ives's oeuvre. But certainly poetry and music in "Ann Street" relate in numerous and witty ways. To list some favorite instances: the gentle, folk-like "quaintness" of the music in Section 2; the abrupt entrance of "Barnums mob" in Section 3, with its jostling grace notes in voice and piano, and the chromatic crowding of the voice on the actual word "mob"; the "narrow" chromatic steps in Section 4; the heavy "feet" in Section 6; the dispirited, directionless "sun" that hits Ann Street in Section 8; and the vocal fall that marks the equally dim "greeting." (This list omits the ending of the song and the climax on "Business," both of which have been alluded to previously.) The blunt, aphoristic character of the text, and its sharp juxtapositions of ideas and images, which help convey the specific meaning of the poem, bear an obvious relationship to the kind of music Ives wrote for it, and to the larger meanings Ives draws from the song through his musical treatment of style and form. Ives's compositional approach is clearly and brilliantly appropriate for this poem, and vice versa, which is doubtless why he was attracted to it.

Henry and Sidney Cowell, in their remarkably insightful early study, *Charles Ives and His Music,* offer the following observations, which apply equally to "Ann Street" in particular and to the large issue of program music in Ives's output:

> Ives is often supposed devoted to program music . . . Actually it [his music] never follows stories nor imitates sounds literally for more than a moment. These extra-musical ideas are rather a jumping-off place, an observation point for the behavior of things in the universe. For Ives the meaning of an event seems to lie in the behavior of the elements that create it, and when he wants to convey an emotion about something, he reproduces the behavior of the sounds that are associated with it, their

approach and departure, their pace and drive, interweaving and crossing—
all this by analogy, which seems to be the way he approaches reality,
rather than by description or literal imitation. . . . Often he does
reproduce several aspects of reality as he first observed them, but from
their behavior he establishes the musical treatment, carrying the ideas
gained from this kind of observation forward to make a system of musical
behavior out of something first perceived on a quite different level.

I must be aware of certain questions and objections that might be raised
about what I have written here. There are surely architectural "flaws" in
the arch of "Ann Street." Among the most obvious are these: Sections 2
and 9 do not use a directly analogous, let alone identical, collection of
pitches; the status of Section 5 as keystone of the arch is compromised by
the status of Section 1 as an introduction, which creates a structural asymmetry (Section 1 should "properly" be the first structural section of the
arch, with a role analogous to that of Section 9—or else, Section 9 should
"ideally" be a coda, with Section 8 analogous to Section 2); and the first
of the piano interludes is stylistically continuous with the music that directly
follows it in Section 4, whereas the second piano interlude, instead of
continuing the style of Section 6, departs from it, creating Section 7 and
another, apparently purposeless, asymmetry in the form. (In reference to
this last "flaw," the temptation to "correct" it by simply claiming that mm.
12–15 of the song are all in the *same* style—a not completely untenable
position—certainly exists. If I were more attracted to strict symmetry and
less insistent on fidelity to the way I actually hear the piece, I would probably
succumb to it.) So, even in this little song, Ives reveals himself to be a
"messy" composer!

In Ives's creative work, it seems that the drive to visualize order and
pattern is counterbalanced by the desire to avoid arbitrarily neat curtailment
of the potential for experience and growth. Again the Cowells say it mem-
orably:

> . . . Ives's aim is not to make the form simple and clear, but rather to
> create an underlying unity out of a large number of diverse elements, used
> asymmetrically; he thus relates his music by analogy to the individual's
> experience of life. The sense of unity is not brought about through exact
> repetition, either of motifs or of sections, but is established through
> relationships. And Ives prefers that these relationships should not be too
> obvious. There must always be something for the mind and feeling to
> work on, some new aspect of relationship to be found. If everything is
> self-evident, that spiritual inactivity that Ives so abhors might be induced.

Thus, some of what initially appears to be "messiness" in Ives's work
may actually be a calculated, intentional effect, stemming from the composer's respect for the complexity of art, and life, and for those listeners

who would join him in his exploration of them. Personally, I will confess to being satisfied with the formal relationships and subtleties that I can understand in "Ann Street." And I am more than a little delighted that there remain some things that I cannot, at least as yet, account for totally— things that still strike me as unpredictable and which keep the piece fresh in my mind and ear, poised to bring future hearings, investigations, and surprises. To quote Ives, such anomalies are "seed for next year's planting," and perhaps I shall always have "the pleasure of never finishing" my analysis.

The procedure utilized by Ives in "Ann Street," that of juxtaposing stylistically distinct sections of music in a particular sequence to create both musical form and musical substance, is found in many of his other works, instrumental as well as vocal. The discussions that follow will demonstrate some additional and wider applications of the type of analysis I have just applied to "Ann Street." But first, some further questions and skepticism regarding the analytical process merit further attention.

Analysis and Its Discontents

It would be a serious mistake, and a serious misrepresentation, for me to claim that my discussion of "Ann Street," or of any other work in this book, has as its purpose the establishment of a *system* for analyzing the music of Ives. That Ives composed according to no set systems, and would have disdained any attempt to characterize his music in terms of systems, scarcely needs further elaboration here. What I am offering is a general *procedure*, a method of approaching Ives's treatment of style.

The essence of this procedure lies not in an attitude toward any specific traditional approaches, nor in the discovery of any particular styles which occur in any particular piece by Ives, nor even in the listing and patterning of styles. All this is manner. What is important in any analysis is akin to what is important in the music being analyzed: its contact with *substance*. If I wish for my analyses to be paradigmatic in any sense, it is only in the sense that they proceed from a desire to allow the substance of music to inspire and to directly inform the techniques employed to understand that substance.

The emphasis on substance in this procedure raises the specter of "excess" subjectivity. The experience of substance, be it in the music or in the analysis of that music, is invariably circumscribed by an individual's own feelings and intellect. In downplaying the importance of both generally accepted, *a priori* modes of understanding, and any necessity for systematizing new approaches, it would appear that I am opening the door to a welter of limited, disorganized, purely personal accounts (mine and others') that may achieve scant interaction, and will result in a lack of any unifying perspective on Ives's work. But returning to the example of Ives himself, and that of his music, may help put some of these misgivings to rest.

Ives was the most personal and idiosyncratic of composers, yet it was his very fidelity to his own unique conception of musical substance that led to a body of work which has come to be so uniquely, profoundly meaningful and challenging to others. Perhaps Ives's overriding characteristic as an artist was his embrace and encouragement of diversity. Hence, any approach to the analysis and discussion of Ives's music that would seek basically to discover systems and to impose limited modes of understanding would also seem inevitably at odds with the music itself. Ives, I think, would have encouraged a multitude of distinctive approaches to his music, and would have welcomed a veritable chorus of probing and questioning voices, both juxtaposed and simultaneous, just as he welcomed the widest array of styles and simultaneities in his music. Fearing no apparent chaos, he would have been confident that it is just through such diversity that new underlying unities will emerge—exactly as such unities emerged in his music. In other words, Ives's work suggests, among many other things, aesthetically consistent ways to go about discussing and analyzing it.

What follows from all this is simply that any personal, honest approach to Ives's work is valid; and, not so simply, any personal, honest approach may also possess at least the seeds of wider truths. Of course, should anyone find that more traditional—or more radical, or merely different—methods of analysis serve better to illuminate Ives's music than the methods put forward in this book, that person should pursue, or create, the indicated model. That would be following my intended paradigm in the fullest and truest sense, without following the manner of my own method in the slightest. Differing methods and emphases are clearly desirable; the validity of any particular manner is neither definitively established by concurrence nor destroyed by the assertion of other approaches. Indeed, the validity of a given approach may lie most in its serving as an impetus to the creation of other, possibly wider-ranging, approaches. In stating this, I am again evoking the spirit of Ives directly, who concluded his *Essays Before A Sonata* with the statement that one man's music may well fall short of its intended goal, especially if that goal is lofty, "but the greater the distance his music falls away, the more reason that some greater man shall bring his nearer those higher spheres."

Ives demonstrates to us that pursuing the personal can bring us closer to the universal. However, attempts to find the universal, especially through a highly abstract, self-consciously "objective" process, may all too often lead to results that are not meaningful in the experience of any single individual. This is a frequent pitfall even of apparently very sophisticated analysis. Ives claimed in the epilogue to his *Essays Before A Sonata* that "eclecticism is part of his [a man's] duty" and that "everyone should have the opportunity of not being over-influenced." He also wrote approvingly elsewhere in the same book of an Emerson who "wrings the neck of any law that would become exclusive and arrogant, whether a definite one of metaphysics or an indefinite one of mechanics." Those who find themselves encouraged by Ives's work to stray from traditionally accepted paths of analysis may take aid and comfort from Ives's reported response to a friend who asked why he didn't write more traditional music: "I can't do it!—*I hear something else!*"

Ives was apparently very reluctant to give any specific interpretative advice to aspiring performers of his works. The comments of John Kirkpatrick, who knew Ives and has been closely associated with his music for more than fifty years both as a pianist and as a scholar and editor, are worth quoting in this connection: "Ordinarily his performers had practically carte blanche to do anything they wanted. His supposition was that if your heart was in the right place, and if you were really devoted in an idealistic way to the music itself, anything you did would have a certain validity, comparable to the validity of what he himself would do in the situation." It is inconceivable that Ives would not have extended the same supposition to those who would discuss, analyze, and try to understand his music.

To summarize, we can both understand and emulate Ives best by welcoming and employing multiple analytical *styles* to his work. It is a truism that no single analytical approach can completely embrace and contain any work of art (and no complex of analytical approaches may be able to do that either), but Ives's work forces us to confront the truth of the truism in a more aggressive manner, perhaps, than other work with a more familiar aspect. In any case, analysts of all music, and of all persuasions, can well learn from Ives the virtues of diversity and of the open ending.

3

Juxtaposition and Sequence (II): Other Tone Roads

"Ann Street" was thoroughly explored in Chapter 2 because it so perfectly exemplifies Ives's employment of multiple styles. Yet should this miniature song really be elevated to paradigmatic status? If so, some explanation must be offered for Ives's lavishing of his most careful, complex, and characteristic musical techniques upon material like Maurice Morris's little newspaper poem.

The explanation lies in the fact that "Ann Street" is a *journey* piece, a work that represents physical and psychological progression. Ives's score makes abundantly clear the progression he understood in the poem. The music gives that progression an obvious physical reality through its employment of "walking" rhythms, and it enhances the progression's psychological implications through the juxtaposition and sequence of styles. By the time we reach the end of the song, we have traversed "Ann Street" physically from its intersection with raucous Broadway to its rather abrupt end. In the process we have learned about it (and *from* it) so that we are intellectually in a different position as well.

The idea of journey, and of progression—physical, psychological, and ultimately spiritual—is of supreme importance in the work of Ives. A great many of his works allude to physical progressions, in the form of walks, marches, or parades. Looking at his songs alone, these range from miniatures like "Ann Street" and "Resolution" to big, extroverted pieces like "Old Home Day" and "The Circus Band," and culminate in the gigantic ambition and achievement of "General William Booth Enters Into Heaven." In "Booth," arguably Ives's greatest song and indisputably one of his major accomplishments in any medium, the imaginary physical journey functions as a metaphor for a spiritual journey and transformation, in which the listener is invited to join. This extraordinary song, which will be discussed below, makes utterly explicit what is almost always implicit in any of Ives's physical journey pieces: that bodily movement from one place to another is ideally accompanied by—should ultimately, in fact, be accompaniment *to,* and metaphor for—progression and development of mind and heart, the broadening of human understanding and empathy. It is not surprising that one of Ives's earliest characteristic songs is entitled (and about) "Walking." (And perhaps it is not merely an accident that the earliest of the songs Ives allowed to survive is a "Slow March," which he composed when he was twelve or thirteen and much later placed as the last of *114 Songs.*)

A list of Ives's important instrumental works inspired by physical journeys would run very long indeed, and would range from chamber pieces like *Over the Pavements* and *Calcium Light Night* to works of the scope and import of "Decoration Day" from the *Holidays* Symphony and "The 'St. Gaudens' in Boston Common" from *Three Places in New England.* It is characteristic that Ives described what is probably his most ambitious single instrumental movement, the stupendous scherzo of the Fourth Symphony, in these terms: "An exciting, easy and worldly *progress* through life is contrasted with the trials of the Pilgrims in their *journey* through the swamps and rough country" (italics added). Equally significant is the fact that the finale of this symphony, which Ives recognized (and many others have since recognized) as one of his consummate spiritual statements, is in the form of a march, with an independent percussion section that keeps the rhythm moving throughout.

If we expand our definition of journey to include those involving water, it adds to the list such important songs as "The Swimmers," "A Farewell to Land," and "The Housatonic at Stockbridge" (as well as the eponymous orchestral piece from *Three Places in New England*). We may also add pieces where the journey is expressed only in philosophical, psychological, or spiritual terms, without an explicit physical counterpart: those remarkable stream–of–consciousness songs like "The Things Our Fathers Loved" and "Tom Sails Away," as well as works of religious meditation and revelation like *Psalm 90.* Works that represent "special cases," drawing on descriptions

34

of, or metaphors for, movement and progression in unusual ways constitute yet another subcategory. This last subcategory would include unique songs like "The See'r" and "The Cage," and a movement like "The Call of the Mountains" from Ives's Second String Quartet. Finally, it should be noted that Ives called two of his non-programmatic but most musically challenging chamber pieces "Tone Roads." In all of the works mentioned, and in many others, the journey is communicated most profoundly not through a title, a text, or a program, but by Ives's *music*—and most typically by Ives's handling of musical style.

Ives's journeys are not typically marked by absolute points of departure or of destination, rather by points of reference along what is ideally a continuing path. This is why Ives's works so often have either indefinite, amorphous kinds of beginnings, or "open" endings, or both. Ives spoke of truth as an "activity," not as a specific, realizable goal that would engender a state of repose; the latter condition, one senses clearly, would be for Ives utterly foreign to anything connected with a search for truth. It is important to remember this in exploring further works, both for the general illumination this conception of truth casts on Ives's aesthetic procedures and desired results, and for the clear warning it provides—especially to analysts and critics.

Ives composed (or completed) the song "Walking" in 1902, and it has already been cited as one of his earliest "mature" songs. A discussion of important aspects of this song, with references to comparable features in the much later "Ann Street," should further illustrate my approach to style in Ives's work, and should also reveal some of the artistic distance Ives traveled in the years between his creation of "Walking" and his creation of "Ann Street" in 1921.

Ives wrote the text for "Walking" and for many of his other songs. It is worth pausing over this text for a moment:

WALKING

A big October morning,
the village church-bells,
the road along the ridge,
the chestnut burr and sumach,
the hills above the bridge
with autumn colors glow.

Now we strike a steady gait,
walking towards the future,
letting past and present wait,
we push on in the sun,

Now hark!
Something bids us pause
> (down the valley,—a church,—a funeral going on.)
> (up the valley,—a road-house, a dance going on.)

But we keep on a-walking,
'tis yet not noonday,
the road still calls us onward,
today we do not choose
to die or to dance,
but to live and walk.

Ives's words directly demonstrate a relationship to his view of life as process rather than product, as journey rather than destination. From the first words, we are thrust into the center of an immediate experience, without preamble or any gradual gathering of intensity, and the deliberately inconclusive ending leaves us with only the continuing journey as our goal. It is indeed, literally, *our* goal, as Ives's use of the first person plural throughout the song invites and involves us viscerally in its action.

The complete score of "Walking" is shown in Ex. 3–1. Major stylistic sections are labeled with numbers, and important musical motives with letters. The song begins with a fairly extensive piano introduction, and concludes with a brief coda in which both voice and piano participate. It will be noticed that there are passages in "Walking" that I have called "transitions." These passages serve as transitions between styles, and may be regarded as the Ivesian equivalent of traditional passages of transition between themes or harmonic areas.

There are obvious and important similarities between "Walking" and the much later "Ann Street." Perhaps most significantly, "Walking" presents an overall stylistic pattern akin to that found in "Ann Street." The style of the first principal section in "Walking" (Section 1) is recalled in the ending section (Section 5). Unlike "Ann Street," of course, "Walking" creates this relationship through literal recurrence, which Ives tended to avoid later in his career. As if to compensate for this literal recapitulation, however, "Walking" does veer off into a fresh and unexpected five-measure coda, pointing the music toward new directions not yet heard or experienced, and dissolving any sense of clear tonal boundaries, melodic shape, and metrical articulation. The occurrence of an open ending creates another, important analogy to "Ann Street." The significant quantity of direct recapitulation in "Walking" serves, in fact, to underline the uniqueness and openness of its ending passage, since the implied, expected, "rounded" ending fails to materialize at the last, critical moment.

It would be easy to cite the substantial occurrence of literal repetition in "Walking" as an obviously "early" stylistic feature. In a similar vein, the

EXAMPLE 3–1. Ives, "Walking," complete.

(continued)

(continued)

relatively smooth flow from section to section in this song (abetted by the presence of transitions), and the especially clear motivic, harmonic, and rhythmic relationships among the stylistic sections (forecasted by the piano introduction) facilitating that flow, along with the song's general air of expansive exuberance, all make this piece seem less radically original than

"Ann Street." Nobody could describe "Ann Street" as a smooth or flowing piece, certainly, and Ives conspicuously avoids transitions that might have alleviated the abrupt changes of style in the later song.

I would suggest, however, that the motivic, harmonic, and rhythmic similarities among the sections of "Walking" may represent not so much an "immature" characteristic as an early understanding on Ives's part of how important it is to emphasize other modes of coherence when stylistic unity is being dissolved. Thus, the focus on G in "Walking" may be seen to correspond to the emphasis on the pitch A in "Ann Street"; the clear motives in the former song function perhaps in a manner akin to the preservation and development of certain limited intervallic shapes throughout the latter, and so on. The full realization of Ives's techniques, which completely redefines the relationships among the components of musical construction in "Ann Street" and many other later works, is arguably still just adumbrated in "Walking." Nevertheless, it is significant that traits which appear on the surface to be "conservative" in an early song could be pointing the way toward Ives's most radical rethinking of musical relationships. Ives frequently forces us to re-evaluate our definitions of "conservative" and "radical," along with many of our other ideas.

It might be argued that the stylistic areas in "Walking" come closer to representing substyles than the kinds of dramatic distinctions of style that are found in "Ann Street." Interestingly enough, the presence of transitions in "Walking," while helping to create a smoother flow, also helps to emphasize those stylistic differences that are present between the sections. For instance, the sense of stylistic difference between Sections 1 and 2 of "Walking" emerges much more clearly after the chromatic transition Ives forges between them than it would have if the two sections simply followed one another directly. The fresh sound of the modal music on G in Section 2, along with Ives's absolute restriction of pitch material in this section to the notes of a scale with a sharped fourth degree and a flatted seventh, emerges baldly and creates a strong feeling of stylistic shift in the context provided by Ives.

Areas of solo piano music are as important in "Walking" as they are in "Ann Street," and they function in analogous ways. These areas serve both to introduce new stylistic sections (as in the measures immediately preceding "Now we strike a steady gait") and to embody entire stylistic sections of the piece (as in the page of piano solo that describes the funeral and the dance, constituting two distinct sections of "Walking"). The extensive piano introduction is worthy of detailed attention.

This introduction anticipates and parallels the opening words by thrusting us directly into a vortex of musical activity. From a conventional standpoint, the music seems to start in the middle, rather than at the beginning of things. The chromatic and dissonant opening two measures give way

41

first to the material labelled *A* in Example 3–1, which has an ambiguous mixed B major-minor character. Then all of this music is shown to be "derived" from the basically diatonic material, suggesting G major, that is labelled *B* in the example. The *B* material substitutes perfect fifths and fourths for the tritones of the opening two measures, and presents an unambiguous G–major coloring (albeit with Lydian influence) in place of the more complex harmony of the *A* material. The *B* material literally anticipates the music of the vocal entrance with its big, clear, diatonic melody line.

Many of Ives's pieces give the impression of starting in the midst of "development" sections, rather than commencing with traditional "expositions." However, in the case of "Walking," and in many analogous passages elsewhere in Ives, the ordering of events is actually inviting us to rethink these traditional notions. After all, *B* derives as clearly from the opening two measures as they do from *B,* and the vocal entrance is as much an enlarged echo of *B* as *B* is an anticipation of that vocal entrance. If we hear it in this unconventional fashion, as Ives compositionally invites us to do, the opening two measures can be apprehended as a "superfluid" of basic musical particles—intervals and rhythmic ideas—that are only later differentiated, and built up, into highly specific melodic, harmonic, and rhythmic complexes. The radical implications of this are obvious; in this interpretation, the seemingly "simpler" ideas are made to appear as the later, more complex results of "development." Ives thus encourages us to rehear, rethink, and re-evaluate some of our most fundamental interpretations of aural experience.

The piano introduction in "Walking" has a function directly analogous to that of the piano introduction in "Ann Street": that of putting forward basic ideas to be utilized in the stylistically diverse main sections of the song to follow. Characteristically, the opening two measures never recur literally in the piece, although they contain the essential material from which the rest of the song is fashioned. If the introduction to "Walking" consisted only of the first two measures of piano solo, the analogy to "Ann Street" would be exact. The ensuing introductory passages in "Walking" expose material that will recur literally in the main sections of the song— namely, material *A* (later the "funeral" music, with a slower tempo and a slight rhythmic alteration), and of course material *B*. In the early song, then, Ives spells out for the listener the function of the introduction; by the time of composing "Ann Street," he was using more subtle, elliptical, and oblique formal methods.

It should be noted that the extensive piano introduction to "Walking" presents more than just basic musical ideas to the listener. It presents stylistic juxtapositions, and in so doing predicts, and presents in microcosm, the formal strategy of the whole piece. This is something the terse introduction to "Ann Street," which is stylistically unified and somewhat distinct from anything else in the piece, cannot do. It is also worth observing that the earlier song's introduction has an open ending, as it deliberately by-passes its G-major cadence two measures before the voice's entrance and hurries off headlong in new directions. In this respect, too, it anticipates the behavior of the piece as a whole. There is no lack of formal originality and subtlety here, despite the presence of more conventional features than may be found in "Ann Street." By the time he had reached his late twenties, Ives had not only discovered a new approach to musical style, he had also already begun to work out internally consistent forms through which to present this approach.

There are additional aspects of "Walking" worthy of comment here, which also anticipate compositional ideas Ives developed more extensively in later works. In the extended piano solo of stylistic Sections 3 and 4, notice that the "dance" initially emerges very gradually out of the "funeral" music, and comes into focus in a virtually cinematic fashion. (Terms like "focus" and "cinematic" suggest themselves frequently when one is at-tempting to describe stylistic and formal patterns found in the mature music of Ives.) Even more strikingly, the dance music of Section 4 is momentarily *overlapped*, while fading out, with the re-entrance of the B material from the piano introduction, which signals the end of our "pause" and the resumption of the mood and purpose of our initial walk. This hint of the overlapping of two distinct musics in "Walking" is a brief, tantalizing adumbration of the "layering" of styles, one of Ives's most distinctive and important contributions to the development of musical forms and textures in the twentieth century.

The way in which Ives fashions convincing forms through progressions of juxtaposed musical styles may of course be illustrated by his instrumental music, as well as by his songs. Let us consider two works: the Scherzo for Chamber Orchestra called *Over the Pavements*—a mature instrumental jour-ney piece which, like "Ann Street," bristles with spiky sonorities and is liberally seasoned with a sense of irony—and the early, well-known *Vari-ations on "America"*—a work as full of youthful exuberance and suggestions of remarkable maturity as "Walking."

Over The Pavements was apparently composed between 1906 and 1913, inspired (again like "Ann Street") by the sounds and rhythms of the busy New York City streets Ives knew so well. It is atypical among works of Ives's maturity for the quantity of literal repetition in it, but this very repetition makes the formal pattern of its various styles especially clear; in this sense, it has a certain kinship to "Walking." Perhaps the amount of repetition is due to the scherzo character of the work, as Ives may have had in the back of his mind, as a point of reference, the traditionally repetitive scherzo-trio-scherzo form.

The piece presents a stylistic arch, like both of the songs considered thus

43

far. The arch may be represented in the simplest way as *A-B-C-B-A*, where the *C* section is the optional cadenza (which Ives labels "To play or not to play"). The perfect symmetry of the basic overall pattern remains even if the cadenza is not played, in which case an even simpler (and very traditional) *A-B-A* form results—although a natural tendency to subdivide the long, repeated *B* section stylistically will be experienced more strongly by the listener when the distinctive cadenza is absent.

The opening measures of each stylistic section are illustrated in Ex. 3–2. As is only appropriate in a work inspired largely by rhythmic phenomena, rhythmic differentiation plays a large and obvious role in defining stylistic areas. It will also be noticed that the layering of different rhythmic patterns

EXAMPLE 3–2. Ives, *Scherzo: Over The Pavements,* mm. 1–5; 32–37; 81–86.

Copyright © 1954 by Peer International Corporation.
Used by Permission.

(*continued*)

upon one another is an aspect of all three of the work's major styles. In both Sections *A* and *B*, an initial passage with two superimposed rhythms is further complicated by the addition of a third, conflicting rhythmic layer (in each case articulated by the trumpet and clarinet in pungent seconds); the rhythms utilized in section *B* are all different from any of the patterns emphasized in section *A*. The cadenza offers yet another pattern, of steady sixteenth notes in the piano, against which a passage composed of progressively shorter note values—also unlike anything else that appears in the piece—is presented by the clarinet, bassoon, and trumpet.

The literal repetition of *A* section material toward the end of the work raises the specter of a "closed" form, but Ives avoids this in a wonderfully humorous and paradoxical fashion by adding a very conventional-sounding two-measure coda in C major (see Ex. 3–3). This conclusion sounds so magnificently "wrong" in this context that it functions like another kind

of Ivesian open ending. In a musical language based on stylistic contrast, where no uniform or normative style can be assumed, context of course is everything—a discovery that Ives utilizes very effectively here. The C–major ending fades quickly, leaving its final G in the bass unresolved. Locally, this creates an effect of amusing incompleteness, akin to the effect the final two measures create in terms of the language of this work as a whole.

Digression (to read or not to read)

The cadenza passage in *Over The Pavements* is the type of thing that tends to get certain people very excited about Ives—I think, for the wrong reasons. It is one of several passages that gets cited as an instance of Ives's "proto-serial" thinking: The piano presents certain widely-spaced chromatic progressions over and over again,

(continued)

in ways that suggest inversions and retrogrades; the wind instruments have a "rhythmic series" in which values of seven, six, five, four, three, and two sixteenth notes successively appear, presented as intervals of sevenths, sixths, fifths, fourths, thirds, and seconds, respectively; as the note values in the winds get progressively shorter, the *number* of notes representing that particular duration gets progressively larger, so that we have four values of seven sixteenth-notes' duration followed by five values of six sixteenth-notes' duration, followed by six values of five sixteenth-notes' duration, and so on.

Actually, considering the rather soulless number play involved, the passage doesn't sound too bad, but surely its lack of real importance to Ives is betrayed by the optional performance status he clearly accorded it. It's an ear- and finger-stretching exercise, spiritually akin to those Ives's father presented to him, and certainly

47

not to be taken too seriously. It belongs to the category of Ives's self-conscious "experiments." Such passages represent, to my way of thinking, the *least* significant aspect of Ives the creator. They attest to his conceptual inventiveness, but they lack that profound quality of true *musical* invention found so often elsewhere in his output, in those passages and pieces where the drive for expression and meaning is paramount over any interest in arbitrarily engendered sound phenomena, and where technique is subservient to content. In the cadenza, unfortunately, manner predominates over substance.

The *Variations on "America"* is the earliest substantial instrumental work by Ives to have survived in anything like its original form. It was composed in 1891 for organ solo, and is still performed by organists, but is now perhaps better known through the clever orchestral arrangement made after Ives's death by composer William Schuman. This early work is worth

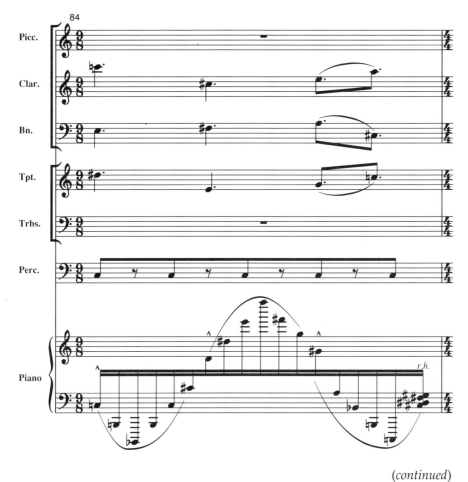

(*continued*)

pausing over, despite its extreme conventionality by Ives's later standards. For one may observe in this precocious early piece a significant foreshadowing of Ives's later compositional concerns and methods. (In referring to the work's conventionality, I am for the moment ignoring the two brief "ad lib." interludes Ives included in the piece, which were probably added at a later date, and which are surely *not* conventional. They will be discussed briefly later.)

Each of Ives's variations is stylistically very distinct from any of the others. Of course, the differentiation of variations within a set through the employment of distinctive substyles can be found in the work of many "old masters." But even though all of the styles Ives explored in the individual

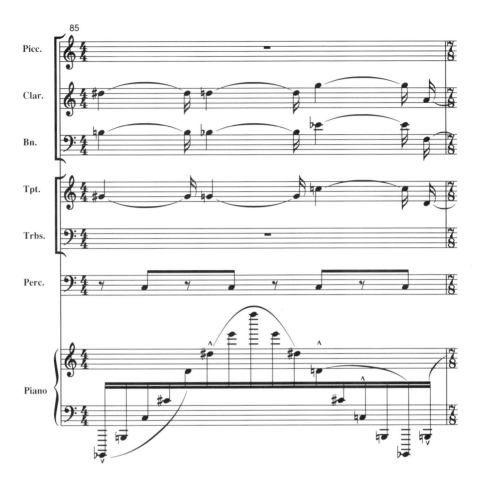

variations of his *Variations on "America"* can be heard as substyles within eighteenth- and nineteenth-century "common practice," there is no question that the seventeen-year-old composer deliberately took both his styles and the differences among them to humorous extremes.

What is significant here is that Ives, before discovering his own distinctive approaches to musical language and formal process, was drawn to a traditional format that enabled and invited him to emphasize and manipulate aspects of style, while maintaining continuity through melodic resemblances and harmonic unity. The analogy to his later works, which demonstrate stylistic diversity applied to a delimited range of motivic, intervallic, and harmonic material, is apparent.

There is also a clear attempt in the *Variations* at shaping the overall

progression of styles; such shaping is, of course, a central concern in Ives's later work. After the stately, purely diatonic presentation of the "America" theme, the first two variations maintain a moderate tempo while demonstrating steadily increasing chromaticism. The third and fourth variations quicken the tempo while retreating to occasional ornamental chromaticism, and the final variation offers a climax of both tempo and chromatic involvement. Additional details in the formal design of these *Variations* strikingly anticipate the later Ives. The work is framed by an introduction—which precedes the theme itself and foreshadows it motivically—and a coda, which flows directly from the material of the final variation. The coda restates material from the introduction, and in recalling the work's point of origin, utilizes a unifying procedure of a type that would become extremely important in many of the later stylistically heterogeneous works.

EXAMPLE 3–3. Ives, *Scherzo: Over The Pavements,* mm. 125–129.

The imprint of the mature iconoclast is surely incipient in the work of the teenager.

There are two hilarious bitonal interludes in the *Variations,* marked "ad lib." by Ives—one between the second and third variations and the other between the fourth and fifth variations—which hint at the way in which Ives would come to use layering to produce new, composite styles. In the first interlude, Ex. 3–4, a diatonic stream of chords presenting the theme in F major is exactly imitated an octave and a major third below, in D♭. Two diatonic chord streams, linked by imitation, thus combine together to pro-

EXAMPLE 3–4. Ives, *Variations on "America"*, mm. 76–79.

Copyright © 1949 Mercury Music Corporation.
Used By Permission Of The Publisher.

duce a style of radically novel character. There is harmonic logic in this as well, since F major is the "old" key of the introduction, theme, and first two variations, while D♭ is the coming key of the third variation. In the interlude, then, both keys are present, perhaps vying for dominance and creating a most original kind of "transition." The organ pedal part adds to the harmonic dualism, oscillating between D♭ and a C, which can be heard either as the leading tone in D-flat major or as the fifth scale degree in F major. In the second interlude, an analogous sense of bitonality is induced, as the four-flat orientation of the fourth variation is set at odds with the F major home key which is to return in variation five.

These interludes suggest how Ives was able to create new styles by extending old styles and procedures in ways that demonstrate a clear internal logic but which were never before associated with such styles or procedures. I am reminded here of similar inventions in Ives's other works of the 1890s: his four-voiced fugues in four keys, or the "enlarged plain chant" of *Sixty-Seventh Psalm*. The latter piece sets two individual harmonic systems moving together, in a fashion certainly more sophisticated than that found in the interludes of *Variations on "America,"* but not completely unlike it. This psalm setting also reveals forcefully how Ives could take a stylistic idea, which might have originated as a joke (as in the interludes of the *Variations*), and shape it for the purposes of intense, expressive musical discourse.

Ives's *Variations on "America"* is clearly important in many ways. It points to significant links, not only between Ives's early work and his own later work, but also between Ives's work and earlier musical traditions. Such links suggest ways of hearing and understanding Ives, which stress the continuity of aspects of his work with more widely accepted musical procedures. Perhaps even more significantly, these links also suggest new ways to hear traditional works, which would emphasize their own continuity with the strikingly new musical visions of Ives.

Influence

A work like the *Variations on "America"* encourages us to look at Ives more closely in terms of the mainstreams of music history and musical style. There are many pieces by Ives that can encourage us to do this, and they are not limited to the compositions of his "immature" years. During and after his studies at Yale, which commenced in 1894 when Ives was approaching twenty, he composed a number of works demonstrating his mastery of various late Romantic idioms. Ives's *114 Songs* offers examples of *lieder* and of French songs, along with songs utilizing more vernacularly-based American styles of the nineteenth and early twentieth centuries. There are even two songs arranged from Ives's cantata, *The Celestial Country,* that reveal the impact which had been made on the young composer by the compositional style of his music instructor at Yale, Horatio Parker. Later in Ives's career, he wrote some pieces in internally consistent modernistic styles, which could well be cited to establish links between Ives and his contemporaries working with avant-garde idioms in Europe.

Ives's own writings reflect his obvious familiarity with, and frequent insight into, much of the standard (and some of the not-so-standard) concert repertoire up through the very early twentieth-century work of Debussy and Richard Strauss; he also, of course, knew and appreciated a wide variety of American musical traditions. In terms of manner, it is clear that Ives absorbed influences everywhere he could. He needed to do this, in fact, to acquire the wide stylistic repertoire that was necessary for his mature work. When existing styles could not serve his expressive purposes, he invented new ones, many of which fit comfortably now within our definition of "modern" musical style. It is thus not difficult to place Ives securely into our standard view of music history, *if* we are content to deal only with individual aspects of his manner.

Of course, it is not his many and various individual manners that define the essence of Ives's contribution and uniqueness—it is the way he used them to express substance. And it is Ives's substance that seems to so elude the search for obvious sources of influence. Where did Ives get his unique conceptions, and the idea of employing stylistic heterogeneity to actualize them? Lacking any obvious answers, we might be inclined to paraphrase Ives himself, and say that his substance comes from—God knows where!

In his writings concerning other composers, Ives expressed most admiration for the substance of Bach and Beethoven. However, he hinted occasionally that he perceived a lack of sufficient stylistic intensity and variety even in the finest of earlier music. Ives reserved the highest praise he offered any musician for one who was not even a composer: his own father. It is in the areas of substance and style that we might best understand the extraordinary influence that Ives attributed to his father.

In Ives's reminiscences, George Ives emerges as a figure of the widest imaginable musical skills, appreciations, and taste—a man with the soundest knowledge of, and respect for, fruitful traditions of all kinds, and also with the most animated interest in any valid experimentation that could extend the expressive possibilities of musical discourse. As his father comes down to us through Ives's writings, he represents a personality in which enthusiasms for cultivated and vernacular music, for conventionally skilled and unschooled but inspired music-making, and for the best of musical traditions along with the most exciting of musical novelties, could exist simultaneously and without any sense of contradiction. Charles Ives put it this way: "What my father did for me was not only in his teaching, on the technical side, etc., but in his influence, his personality, character, and open-mindedness, and his remarkable understanding of the ways of a boy's heart and mind. He had a remarkable talent for music and for the nature of music and sound, and also a philosophy of music that was unusual." It is of no real import here whether this description presents a "true" portrait of George Ives; the nature and importance of the influence as Ives wished to understand it, and as Ives wished others to understand it, is apparent. In his remembrances of George Ives, Charles clearly described for us, among other things, the "ideal listener" toward whom his polystylistic music is directed.

What of Ives's own influence upon later composers? Here, again, it is simple enough to speak about manner, and extremely difficult to discuss substance. When Ives's music first came to be widely known after World War II, "modern" music was already an aging development; the novelty for most people was the stylistic diversity in his work. Many composers were obviously intrigued by the heterogeneity of style in Ives, and an analogous interest in heterogeneity has since manifested itself in the work of a good number of these composers. (This issue has already received some attention in Chapter 1.) Whether the now-prevalent interest in heterogeneity reflects more than a surface kind of influence from Ives is, however, doubtful. It is easy enough to adopt some stylistic diversity and unpredictability into a repertoire of musical techniques, but whether anything like Ives's regard for substance transfigures later polystylistic music by turning technique into communication is a much more complex matter. In some of this music, one is forced to wonder if a feature that constitutes one of the most substantive aspects of Ives's art has not been ironically transformed into merely a superficial "mannerism."

In a generalized sense, Ives's influence may be seen everywhere now—even in the simple diversity of the contemporary musical scene—just as Ives himself absorbed influences from everywhere as a budding composer. But in a more specific and demanding sense, Ives seems to stand in as unique a position in relation to his musical posterity as he does in relation to his musical forebears. He is part of music history, but he also seems to stand a certain distance from it. One might say that Ives is "of" music history, but not fully "in" music history. The nature of his concerns as an artist, and his creative realization of those concerns, appear to set him apart to some degree from the mainstreams of music history and musical style. There will be more to say about these matters later in this book.

4

Mental Journeys (I)

Charles Ives's musical journeys do not always suggest a physical counter-part. "The Things Our Fathers Loved" and "Tom Sails Away" are worthy of attention as two outstanding examples of what I will call Ives's "mental journey" pieces. Both of these songs deal with memory, as a process. Their texts deal with specific memories but, just as in the case of the "physical" journey songs that have been examined, the concrete and personal realities described in the texts are aspects of the manner of these songs and are ultimately made part of, and subordinate to, a larger substance. It is im-portant to remember that Ives, as he wrote in his *Essays Before A Sonata*, was always most interested not in "something that happens, but the way something happens."

In both of these songs, a complex and paradoxical view of memory, and of its psychological role, is presented in Ives's words and music, yielding a complex but integrated aesthetic experience. If I had to reduce Ives's viewpoint to a short verbal summary—which by its very nature could not remotely do that viewpoint justice—I might say that memory, for Ives, is omnipresent in our personalities and necessary for defining who we are and want to be, at the same time that *specific* memories are elusive and eternally fleeting, so that dependence upon them is fruitless. The most memory can do is to inspire us to continually renew and reinvent ourselves in accordance with what we have most valued and achieved in our past. Memory, then, is a tool for forging a meaningfully *active* life.

This is the opposite of nostalgia. Songs like "The Things Our Fathers Loved" and "Tom Sails Away" do provide wonderful demonstrations of that tender side of Ives, which informs much of his music and gives the lie to those who would see him only, or chiefly, as a kind of two-dimensional cartoon figure pounding out dissonances for masculinity's sake. But these songs are absolutely unsentimental. Their avoidance of sentimentality, especially in the face of their surface subject matter, is a profound achievement. These songs reflect how successfully Ives could transform a complicated vision of human reality into artworks that are not only true to his vision but which, through their aesthetic originality and richness, reveal, enhance, and intensify that vision for us. Ives's "mental journeys," whether inspired by memory or by pure imagination, bear the same relationship to his conceptual life as the physical journeys described in so many pieces. They are concerned with the ongoing processes of an active existence whose ultimate goal is spiritual growth. Forms engendered by stylistic juxtapositions are obviously well suited for conveying such processes. They are ill suited for evoking an emotion as essentially passive as nostalgia.

The widespread misperception of Ives as a nostalgic composer is due, I think, to a dual misunderstanding: first, a misunderstanding of Ives's conception and use of memory in his own life and work; and second, a misunderstanding of the techniques Ives utilized in his work to actualize his perception in aesthetic terms. Many issues are opened up here, including Ives's use of quotation, his deliberate evocation of "old" musical styles, and his programmatic subject matter in a number of important instrumental works. For the present, my concern is with the composer's stylistic techniques, but I think an accurate understanding of these will illuminate much.

"The Things Our Fathers Loved," which is shown in Ex. 4–1, shows obvious structural kinships to the physical journey pieces discussed earlier, along with some striking features not previously encountered. The piece clearly presents a sequence of varying styles, ending with a veiled return to the opening material. As in "Ann Street," the return is far from literal, and in fact the ending of the present song disguises its relationship to the song's opening music even more than is the case with "Ann Street," for reasons which should become clear as the character and meaning of "The Things Our Fathers Loved" are examined. As in "Walking," Ives provided his own words for this song.

The sense of stylistic juxtaposition is not nearly as abrupt in this song of memory as in some Ives pieces. This choice on Ives's part is necessitated by the nature of his desired result: a meditative and poignant song. Ives assures this relative smoothness in two ways: first, by utilizing styles that, while varied, are not as divergent in character as in other, more emphatic

EXAMPLE 4–1. Ives, "The Things Our Fathers Loved," complete.

Copyright © 1955 by Peer International Corporation.
Used by Permission.

(continued)

works; and second, through a most artful use of transitional passages between sections in different styles. These transitions function, along with very prominent motivic and textural interrelationships among the sections of the song, to create a highly integrated musical fabric, on both surface

(*continued*)

and deeper levels. Relationships to the much earlier "Walking" are evident here. As in "Walking," the transitions in "The Things Our Fathers Loved" operate in a way that also helps to indicate the stylistic differences between adjacent main sections of the song.

A subdivision of the song into five stylistic sections and transitional passages is indicated directly on the score in Ex. 4–1. What differentiates a transition here from a self-contained stylistic section? Length, for one thing—the transitions last one or two measures only, while the sections are longer—but an even more important factor is the stylistically ambiguous character of these transitions. While each of them (with the exception of the final quasi-transition, which performs its own special role to be dis-

62

cussed later) begins with a significant deviation from the style—in particular, the harmony—of its immediately preceding section, none of them
unequivocally establishes a new stylistic frame of reference. The first three
transitions each seem to serve two functions in quick succession: first, that
of moving away from the currently prevailing style; and second, that of
preparing the listener for the stylistic section to follow, through textural,
harmonic, or other means.

It will be noticed that, beginning with the first transition, each of the
divisions in the score starts with an unexpected movement of a half step
in one or more of the prominent lines in the texture, which creates a striking
shift in the harmony at these points. This kind of effect is all the more
obvious for being substantially avoided within all of the stable stylistic
sections of the piece. It is perhaps anticipated by the chromaticism in the
right hand of the piano part during the first section, but these gentle
disturbances do not occur in rhythmically prominent positions and have
an altogether different effect from the later, division-creating harmonic
surprises. (Perhaps these early "disturbances" are musical hints of the
inexact, unfocused nature of the memory process, something which
emerges more forcefully as the song progresses.)

A glance at the first couple of harmonic "surprises" will illustrate how
they operate in the song. The first transition announces itself with the
movement of the piano's bass line from F, which has just been heard in
m. 3 as a clear subdominant of C major, to an unanticipated and unexplained
F$\sharp$, accompanied with an upward chromatic shifting of the vocal line as
well. The dominant ninth chord on E$\flat$ in the next measure is presented in
piano figuration anticipating that of Section 2, but the A$\flat$ chord it seems
to be preparing never arrives. In its stead is an elaborate harmony built on
A$\natural$, a half step "too high," whose arrival in turn clearly demarcates the
actual arrival of the new section. Succeeding divisions in the piece are
marked by analogous events in the harmony.

The effect of these harmonic shifts is to call attention to the shifting and
elusive quality of the memories being evoked; the effect is strongly sec-
onded, of course, by the stream-of-consciousness character of Ives's words.
This effect is very much like a modern cinematic one, with mental "pictures"
coming in and out of focus. The "camera" cannot remain fixed on its subject;
the image wavers and begins to cloud over almost as soon as it is visualized.

Having established these patterns and effects during the earlier portions
of the piece, Ives is able to build upon them further, with remarkable impact,
from Section 3 to the end of the song. Section 3 presents the "simplest"
style achieved in the piece. Here, both piano and voice are in a clearly
diatonic F major, and indeed this section may be seen as the logical goal
of a process of gradually lessening chromaticism and harmonic complexity
through Sections 1 and 2. However, the "picture" remains subtly askew

in Section 3, due to the rhythmic displacement between the voice and the piano, which results in some peculiar, if diatonic, dissonances. This prevents the piece from moving toward any sense of closure in this section—as does the acceleration of tempo, and the lingering feeling from Section 1 that F is the subdominant of the "main key" of C. A thoroughly unstable measure of transition thrusts us into Section 4, stylistically the most complex and active portion of the entire piece. The fortissimo downbeat of this section obviously marks the climax of the song. The fact that Sections 3 and 4 are separated by a much greater divergence in style than has been encountered previously in the piece also bifurcates the song at this point.

From this point on, memory simply refuses to focus. The apparent movement earlier toward simplicity and traditional unification turns out to be merely a fleeting chimera of the mind. Disjunction now takes over the piece and events proceed toward greater fragmentation and surface disunity, in spite of the climatic call "Now! Hear the songs!"—which is ironically followed by the weakening disclaimer, "I know not what are the words."

Throughout Section 4 to the end of the quasi-transition, the harmonic idiom seems to be moving gradually toward diatonicism again. Section 5 does bring a drastic reduction in textural, rhythmic, and dynamic activity, but it utterly fails to achieve melodic or harmonic resolution or closure. The return to "simplicity" is subverted. With its numerous harmonic and melodic "surprises," Section 5 concludes the song with a poignantly inexact image of the song's opening style and melodic shape.

In certain ways, the second "half" of the song may be heard as presenting a reversed and altered echo of the first "half." Notice the "distorted" references in the upper register of the piano part of mm. 15–18 to the melodic motives of the piano part in Section 3. It could be said that the latter "half" of the song holds up a strange "funny mirror" to the first "half," evoking it and, at points, mimicking it, but being unable to recapture anything truly like the original image—just as the efforts of one's memory to recapture what is past are revealed to be ultimately futile in this song.

From a formal standpoint, "The Things Our Fathers Loved" is an exceedingly sophisticated song, as complex and ultimately unclassifiable as the process of memory it is describing. This is not because it has no real form, but because (again, like memory) it has elements of different structures occurring simultaneously. It has aspects of a two-part form, of an arch-like or "mirror" form, and of a steadily developing "through-composed" form. Style plays a clear role in articulating these diverse formal elements.

The unifying interval throughout "The Things Our Fathers Loved" is clearly the third, which is an omnipresent building block in the vocal line, and which is obviously prominent in the accompaniment, both melodically and harmonically. The third serves Ives's purposes extremely well for a number of reasons. Used melodically, it is evocative of tonality, and of diatonic tunes, almost inescapably; hence the feeling, so frequent in this song, that half-remembered and half-forgotten tunes are being recalled, more or less imperfectly. At the same time, the third is not necessarily tied to any given diatonic scale or tonality. Chords based on thirds can be plain triads, seventh chords of innumerable varieties, lush or highly dissonant ninth chords, and many other constructions for which we have no convenient names. In other words, the third is a wonderful stylistic chameleon.

One remaining area of interest involves the harmonic progression that underlies almost the entire song, and which contributes strongly to its shaping and the emotional effect of its ending. Sections 1 through 4 strongly suggest an overall harmonic plan of very traditional cast, centering upon the tonality of C major.

Section 1 presents a strong tonic to subdominant movement in the harmony; the importance of the F–major subdominant chord in this section is reinforced in Sections 2 and 3, where F assumes the role of a temporary tonic. (It is significantly reinforced in this role by the prominence in these two sections of its own subdominant degree, $B^\flat$.) Section 4, in the vocal part, firmly suggests an orientation around G major, the dominant of C. (The importance of G is also briefly anticipated in the vocal melody at the beginning of Section 2.) So far, the song might clearly imply a big I–IV–V progression, heading for "home" and C major in Section 5.

It is true that G major never actually appears in the harmony of Section 4, a fact that contributes to the feeling of the dissolution of memory in this section, and which makes the ending of the song more convincing in its harmonic irresolution than it might prove otherwise. But an emphasis on fifth relationships throughout Section 4 does provide some minimal continuing support for the expectation that this piece might achieve traditional harmonic integration and closure. At the beginning of the section, there is a powerful feeling in the harmony of D as dominant to an implied G major. In the piano bass line, D is approached by a descent of a fifth from A at the end of the preceding transition, lending further credence to the idea that Ives might be setting up a series of progressions by fifths, A–D–(G), in order to end at last on the C major to which G is the dominant harmony. Section 4 (and/or the quasi-transition) ends with another descent of a fifth in the piano bass line, from B to E. It is still possible at this point to hear the E–minor chord in m. 20 as a momentary deceptive resolution of a strong dominant harmony on D that began Section 4 (that is, as a VI chord in a V–VI progression in G); the aural idea of G major is still alive, if not well.

The reasons for showing a quasi-transition at the end of Section 4 in "The Things Our Fathers Loved" should now be made explicit. Stylistically, the music is gradually becoming more diatonic in mm. 18–20; although

65

"errant" G♯s persist in mm. 18 and 19, the pitches of a G-major scale certainly predominate the aural landscape, and by m. 20, the piano part is utilizing only white keys. Although texture, rhythm, and figuration remain similar throughout these measures, giving a strong feeling of continuity, there is still some sense of a harmonic transition taking place, and by m. 20 Ives certainly seems to be making possible the return of a diatonic C–major pitch collection. The high parallel thirds in the piano here would seem to anticipate the literal return of the song's opening, harmonically and melodically. The aura of "return" is reinforced by the fact that the piano now at last achieves, after many "false" attempts, a literal transposition of its dotted motive from Section 3. In a sense, this fading little motive is the real transitional gesture, but it remains a quasi-transition ultimately because the full return for which it seems to be preparing never takes place. Instead, the transition proves to be a dissolving, fleeting glimpse, as if from the corner of the mind's eye, of a definitive final section and arrival that cannot be achieved. That is why this little area of the song is so important, and why it is impossible to find an unambiguous name and formal description for it.

It would be logical enough, musically, for the vocal line at the start of Section 5 to continue its sequence of descending thirds and sound the E–D–C, which would return the song "home." Instead, a half-step displacement leads from G to F♯—which has its own logic, given the song's earlier behavior—and the voice's opening melody recommences as if in D major. But the piano's arrival is also displaced by a half step, both from the voice and from its own preceding E, yielding an enharmonic E♭ major triad (spelled with D♯ and A♯) of startling poignancy against the voice's D. As if startled itself, the voice "forgets" the repeated pitches of its opening melody line, and begins its ascent, lowering its last two pitches by a half step in an attempt to accommodate the new harmony, and use D♯ as a dominant to a final G♯. The piano part, although obviously attempting some accommodation to the voice by uncharacteristically doubling its melody line, at last lacks the strength to cooperate with the voice in "resolving" the song, and sinks back on a most inconclusive *minor* dominant chord just as the voice presents its purported last-minute tonic. The emotional potential inherent in the combination of a suggested stylistic return with unexpected melodic, harmonic, and rhythmic deviations could not be more movingly realized.

The harmonic behavior of Section 5 echoes that of the song as a whole by bringing us toward an expectation of full closure, and strongly hinting at that closure, but not providing it. The combined sense of hope and loss at the last is intensified, and assured, by Ives's careful notation of a catch-breath just before the final word and chord of the song, and by his call for the softest dynamic level of the entire piece at its conclusion.

66

It should be remarked, in passing, how painstaking Ives can be in his indications to performers. Notice also the important quarter-note rest with which the piano part begins: a "heard" silence of meditation, from the depths of which memory is summoned, and which must be observed in a faithful performance. Some scholars have argued that Ives was habitually careless of the needs of performers and of the effect of his music in performance. Instances like the present ones belie this. The truth is that Ives was "careless" in his notation to performers only in cases where he wanted to encourage them to be a little free and easy with his ideas, and that when he needed performers to respect small details, he provided those details with great care and sensitivity. Ives varied his degree and kind of specific control over performers from piece to piece, and often within pieces, just as he varied his use of style. In fact, he sometimes used this issue of control as an *element* of style. This is a matter to which I will later return.

What at last is the meaning of the ending of "The Things Our Fathers Loved"—perhaps the most deeply poetic of Ives's open endings? Taken by themselves, Ives's words seem reasonably confident and straightforward; the music demands that we look beyond and beneath the surface to "where new horizons wait." The final words of the song may complete a statement, but the music asks a question.

The concluding words state for the first time the song's title. Yet the music forces us to realize that the title is ambiguous, at least in the sense that while the song deals with one person's musical memories, what these memories apparently evoke is not so much something merely personal, but the things our *Fathers* loved. And it is the musical isolation and incompleteness of the word *loved* at the song's ending that points the questioning finger: they *loved*, but do I (we) still *love*? And do we love enough—love our heritage enough to make it into something still living in our thoughts, actions, and lives, rather than something frozen in the past and in the love of those older and perhaps (or soon to be) gone?

As a consequence of Ives's musical treatment, "The Things Our Fathers Loved" thus belongs to a group of what might be called Ives's "question" songs. It doesn't literally state a question, like others in this group (such as "On The Antipodes," "The Cage," and "General William Booth Enters Into Heaven"), but it operates certainly in a way that asks one, or several, questions. This song comes from the period when the United States was entering World War I, which explains much about the tone of questioning remembrance and about the probable import for Ives of the parenthetical subtitle he provided for the song ("and the greatest of these was Liberty"). But it surely is unnecessary to know this historical background to respond to this remarkable meditation on memory, which Ives turns also into a pointed meditation on values.

Traditionalism and Modernism: Nostalgia or "Back to the Future"?

Is Charles Ives ultimately a special kind of traditionalist? I am not in agreement with those who would view Ives primarily as a nostalgic composer, but it is evident that evocations of the life and the values of small-town, late nineteenth-century America play an enormous role in the surface subject matter of his work. This is plainly to be seen in Ives's song texts (and there is no better example of it than "The Things Our Fathers Loved"), in the programs he provided for his instrumental works, and in his writings about his own music. And Ives, of course, frequently evokes the traditional musical languages of this historical America.

On the other hand, when Ives does evoke traditional musical styles, he as frequently as not "distorts" them with "irregularities" of melody, harmony, rhythm, and texture, virtually transforming them into "modern" styles. Again "The Things Our Fathers Loved" may be cited as a fine example of this. Furthermore, throughout his oeuvre, Ives writes in aggressively "modern" musical styles, without any traditional echoes, as often as he utilizes any aspects of tradition—if not more often. Doesn't this make Ives a modernist?

I suspect not. *Webster's Ninth New Collegiate Dictionary* defines modernism as: "a self-conscious break with the past and a search for new forms of expression." Ives searches for new forms of expression, certainly, but he does not consciously *break* with the past at all—he brings the past right along on his search! The virtually exclusive emphasis on newness, on continuously pushing the frontiers of stylistic manner forward, that characterizes modernist art does not characterize Ives's oeuvre. Yet traditionalism ("the doctrines or practices of those who follow or accept tradition") surely doesn't characterize it either. In a sense, Ives certainly accepts tradition, which is why he isn't a true modernist, but he just as certainly doesn't "follow" tradition.

Is Charles Ives then the Janus of American music? His work seems at once traditional and futuristic, but in fact it is neither, and even the Janus image will not do. Ives is interested in the *present*. This is not the present of a particular time, place, person, or culture, rather it is an always extant and ever-changing *artistic* present: the current intellectual, emotional, and spiritual condition of creator, performer, listener—in short, humanity. Ives's music seeks to engage the present as it is being lived and experienced, and to move with and through that present meaningfully into a new present enriched by the experience of the music. Aspects of the past, and potential for the future, are an inescapable part of the present, of course, and Ives's music directly acknowledges this. Yet the goal of his art almost always seems to be that of immersing us more deeply in the experience of the present, rather than in some past experience, real or imagined, or in some imagined future experience.

Thus, it surely is no accident that the text of "The Things Our Fathers Loved" is written in the *present* tense, in spite of the remembered subject matter. In fact, Ives's song texts and programs are almost always written in the present tense. The remembered past is treated as a direct part of the present in other songs such as "Tom Sails Away," "Old Home Day," "Memories," "The Circus Band," "Remembrance," and many additional ones; and elaborate programs for instrumental works having to do with the America of Ives's boyhood and young manhood, such as those for the movements of the *Holidays* Symphony and for *Central Park in the Dark,* are also written as if they are describing the present.

Ives's view of the present is never that of one satisfied with the present; the belief in, and striving toward, continuing progress is too important for him. Far from seeing in the present the end point of any cycle, Ives views it simply as a point of departure from which we must continue to move forward toward greater freedom and spiritual growth—as individuals, as a nation, and as a world. This spiritual orientation, belief in progress, and desire to build upon the best values and achievements of the past are all traits that might suggest some kinships between Ives and today's "neo-conservatives." However, given Ives's historical position, one following this line of thought would have to call him a *pre*-neoconservative.

On the other hand, the composer's willing acceptance of stylistic pluralism distances him strongly from anything with which "neoconservatives" would be comfortable, and links him instead, in aesthetic attitudes at least, with some of the more radical contemporary "post-modernists." Does this make Ives then a *pre*-post-modernist?

It is difficult, arbitrary, and at last fairly useless to place Ives within historically defined movements and contexts. By utilizing traditional and modernistic elements in the same pieces, Ives in effect de-historicizes and de-familiarizes sounds and idioms that we customarily experience as very specific historical, cultural, and stylistic markers. The effect is geometrically multiplied by the way in which Ives tends to "distort" traditional styles and to place his own idiosyncratic spin on "modernistic" styles. Our conventional categories and assurances disappear, and we are more or less forced to confront the music naked, in an immediate present—which, I suspect, is exactly what Ives would have wanted.

Although the small-town America Ives knew and loved has faded into history, his artistic celebration of it has paradoxically become more accessible with the passage of time. As the culture of the world becomes increasingly more heterogeneous and pluralistic, Ives's work becomes increasingly more relevant. It is this wondrous phenomenon to which Aaron Copland referred so movingly when he wrote of Ives's "gamble with the future that he has miraculously won."

5

Mental Journeys (II)

"Tom Sails Away" is a song that shares with "The Things Our Fathers Loved" music of cinematic scene-shifting qualities and a stream-of-consciousness text by Ives, both of which evoke the process of remembering. In each of these songs, the music intensifies the specific memories being described and underlines their evanescent aspect.

"Tom Sails Away" was composed during the same year as "The Things Our Fathers Loved," and was even more obviously inspired by World War I. The memories here are specifically those of childhood, and the tone is intensely personal. The complete score of "Tom Sails Away" is shown as Ex. 5–1. The tenderness of feeling and the sensitivity to nature and detail in both text and music can lead us into stereotyping the singer/narrator, Tom's sibling, as female, especially since the one remembering is left behind as Tom sails off. However, there is no more necessity of making this assumption than there is of being surprised that a song like this could come from such a "masculine" composer as Ives. As specific as the song's surface may be, it probes feelings and issues that are not specific as to time, place, or gender. As in "The Things Our Fathers Loved," the ultimate subject matter of "Tom Sails Away" is the nature of memory.

The design and compositional techniques of "Tom Sails Away" are significantly akin to those found in "The Things Our Fathers Loved," and an investigation of them will provide a further illustration of how Ives constructs mental journeys with stylistic juxtapositions. As memory shifts from detail to detail in "Tom Sails Away," stylistic shifts in the music illuminate the progression of thought, ultimately creating larger patterns within the seemingly spontaneous flow of ideas. Usually, the musical movement from

EXAMPLE 5–1. Ives, "Tom Sails Away," complete.

From: Nineteen Songs.
Copyright © 1935 Merion Music, Inc.
Used By Permission Of The Publisher.

Second Major Section

Faster and more animated

(continued)

one stylistic area to the next in "Tom Sails Away" is accomplished—once again—by striking half-step shifts in the voice part or harmony, or in both at once. There are many short stylistic sections in this piece; the musical example shows only the major points of formal articulation.

We again find the presence of an implied harmonic center—in this case, on F$^\sharp$—that dominates much of the song but which is evaded at the ending.

There is the feeling of a stylistic arch created by the return of the opening melody and chord structures in the song's final measures; this is a varied return that creates yet another of Ives's open endings.

The strong climax a little more than halfway through the song (at the words "Daddy is coming up the hill from the mill"), set apart by the faster tempo, by the high point in the vocal line, and by the intensity of rhythmic activity in the accompaniment, suggests a bifurcation in the overall form of the piece. This suggestion is supported by other details of structure, which will be discussed; we have here another analogy to "The Things Our Fathers Loved." In addition, the music of "Tom Sails Away" is dominated by the recurring use of particular intervallic patterns, in this case based upon fourths and fifths, which points up its relationship to all the Ives songs discussed previously. The intervals chosen, as in "The Things Our Fathers Loved," enable Ives to introduce musical quotations into the fabric of the song with the utmost smoothness and sense of logic.

Unlike "The Things Our Fathers Loved," "Tom Sails Away" has a brief piano introduction. This introduction is analogous to those in "Ann Street" and "Walking." The piano puts forward intervallic patterns that bear a generative relationship to the melodic and chordal materials used throughout the main body of the song. There is also a direct relationship here between the piano introduction and the music that immediately ensues, as the introduction clearly foreshadows the opening melody in the voice; see the brackets in Ex. 5–1.

The second measure of "Tom Sails Away" establishes the song's "home" area of F$\sharp$ with a diatonic collection of pitches that suggests F$\sharp$ minor with a natural seventh degree. The folk-like, modal feeling of this opening is atypical for Ives, but perfectly evocative of the distant simplicity of childhood. The musical idiom becomes more complex almost immediately, then returns briefly to a diatonic collection, stressing intervals of fifths and fourths in the piano and a stepwise whole-tone idea in the voice, to portray the setting sun. At this point, the crucial scene preparation has been accomplished, and a vision of the family is introduced, as "mother with Tom in her arms" appears.

Although styles continue to change rapidly—a characteristic of this song throughout its duration—it is possible to hear a large portion of the song, which begins with the first reference to "mother" and ends just before the first reference to "daddy," as one self-contained formal area, to which all the music preceding serves as an extensive introduction. This is possible for musical reasons as well as purely textual ones. At the end of this formal area, the piano restates the motive of "mother with Tom in her arms," which is heard in the vocal part at the beginning of this large section. (The motive and its restatement are indicated in Ex. 5–1.) The restatement is accompanied by the return of the F$\sharp$ pedal point in the piano bass line, which has been essentially absent since the opening measures of this formal area. Other unifying aspects in this large area of the song are the unchanging tempo and the relatively straightforward rhythmic patterns. These contribute to the peaceful, slow-moving character of the scene being portrayed. The musical character alters radically with the arrival of "daddy."

The animated depiction of daddy's return home creates a second major section in the song, a section seemingly foreshortened textually and musically at the narrator's abrupt return to the reality of "today," when Tom has gone off to war. At this point, tempo, texture, harmony, and melodic and rhythmic character all change suddenly, in a way that is familiar in much of Ives's music, but which is particularly effective in this context. The effectiveness is significantly due to the psychological truth Ives captures here through his treatment of style. The narrator's completed vision of family togetherness cannot be maintained in the face of the family's present fragmentation. Yet the foreshortening of the second major section comes to make musical and formal sense as well, because the passages describing Tom's departure for "over there," which follow the imagined appearance of daddy, create a roughly symmetrical parallel to those scene-setting passages that *precede* the appearance of mother in the dream landscape. If the earlier passages set the scene, the later ones effectively destroy it; and of course the sense of symmetry is enhanced at the end of the song by music and words that recall the very beginning.

The symmetry of design in "Tom Sails Away" would be more "perfect" if the section describing daddy lasted longer, but it should be clear by now that, for Ives, the goal of achieving psychological depth and fidelity is inherently more meaningful than the goal of achieving an abstract ideal of aesthetic "perfection." The action and intensity of the music at daddy's arrival are true to the remembered moment. The "too-rapid" dissipation of that music is not only psychologically true to the narrator's *present* moment, but is formally appropriate in the sense that any "imbalance" resulting from the dissipation serves as a structural representation of memory's ultimate failure to freeze time and space. Tom's departure has skewed the perfection and symmetry of the narrator's world. The revelation of that departure in the song is the point at which the form of the piece itself becomes "skewed."

The differences between the opening vocal passage of "Tom Sails Away" and the roughly parallel ending passage are important and wonderfully expressive. Musically, the opening passage is displaced a half step downward at the end. This will be experienced as a darkening effect even by casual listeners, and the lowering, darkening feeling is underlined by the final fading repetitions in the voice part of the note C, the lowest note sung in the piece. Listeners with an acute sense of pitch will strongly feel the harmonic incompleteness of the ending—especially because of the strong periodic returns to F♯ throughout the song and because the song comes so close to a full cadence in F♯ major in the passage just preceding these ending measures. At the end, both voice and piano seem to vaporize and disappear before our very ears, "floating" away like the visions described by the singer/narrator, as the song fades into inaudibility rather than truly concluding.

One must also marvel at Ives's choice of words to end his piece. Initially the scenes from childhood were "with" the protagonist—the choice of preposition effectively indicating closeness and security, perhaps even implying possession or at least some degree of control by the narrator. At the end, the remembered visions no longer seem within the singer's control, as they have become insubstantial and diaphanous, evaporating, *floating* before the essentially passive eyes of one who is helpless to retain them. Such attention to verbal as well as musical detail is indicative of one who has mastered every aspect of the craft of songwriting.

The open ending of "Tom Sails Away" is anticipated by the absence of firm concluding musical gestures at any of the internal points of subdivision in the song. This, as we have seen, is typical of Ives's approach to form. In connection with this, I might call particular attention to the striking passage just before the coda, the "almost" cadence in F♯ (or G♭) major, where the right hand of the piano refuses to cooperate fully with the implied cadential arrival of the voice and the left hand of the piano.

Ives is dealing with some fascinating musical, textual, and psychological complexities at this point. For "over there" is Tom's point of arrival, but "over there" are also the reasons for his departure from the narrator, and for the uncertainty of the future. The boisterous, affirming quality of the quoted war tune "Over There" is ironically at odds with the mood of Ives's song even as it is being recalled. At the rather lugubrious tempo in which Ives actually presents it, the stalwart cadence figures of "Over There" may evoke in fact the finality of Tom's distance from the protagonist and the feared finality of death, which could cause him never to return. Thus, Ives at once presents his quotation and reinterprets its original flavor and meaning; verbally, through the total context in which it is presented, and musically, through the local use of an "inappropriate" tempo and the addition of extraneous, "inappropriate" pitches in the right hand of the piano part, which render this moment richly ambiguous and poignant. The quotation itself is beautifully chosen to assure that its words and music will make the necessary aesthetic points to one who does not recognize the tune or does not even recognize that something is being quoted. How admirable that Ives manages to use a stylistic "mannerism," a quoted tune, in such a way that it reflects directly on the *substance* of the piece!

It could be asserted further that this deliberate "distortion" of a quoted tune penetrates directly to the conceptual core of "Tom Sails Away" by providing yet another illustration of the way in which the present acts upon the processes and subjects of memory. Ives shows us in this memorable song that nothing remembered—be it a hit tune from the present or a profound childhood memory from the distant past—can retain its original shape, hold, and meaning in light of the inevitable changing flow of life's events.

Quotation: Personal, "All-American," or Universal?

Ives's use of the quoted tune "Over There" in his song "Tom Sails Away" demonstrates how his quotations may be woven directly into the substance and meaning of a piece, in such a way as to actually enhance that substance and meaning. It also demonstrates an aspect of Ives's art that has not received enough attention. His employment of quotation is often most interesting *not* because of the external references suggested by it, but because of the *internal* relationships it creates in his works.

Ives's music looks outward to the world, of course, but it looks outward as a whole, not as small segments. It looks toward the widest possible perspective rather than toward narrow, specific references. The more we appreciate the function of a quoted passage in the stylistic structure and in the aesthetic implications of an Ives piece, the less important it may become to know it is a quoted passage at all. We might say that Ives works, on all levels, to suppress his quotation marks—to make his quoted material truly his own.

These statements are by no means intended to suppress interest in Ives's use of quotations. Those scholars engaged in identifying Ives's quoted tunes and the personal and cultural associations Ives might have had with those tunes are, in fact, helping in a significant way to preserve a very valuable part of America's heritage that is in increasing danger of becoming far too unknown and obscure. But it needs to be stressed that, in terms of specific relevance to an understanding of Ives's *music*, the mere identification of quotations and associations can only be a starting point. Quotations may provide some, even much, of the raw material for an individual composition, but they are *not* the composition itself, any more than a tone row or a major scale is a composition. Hearing quotations is not hearing a composition, and listing quotations is not analyzing a composition. The interest must lie in how the composer uses the material to make an aesthetic statement. And quotations provide only one of many suitable starting points for an investigation of this.

It could be argued that when Ives was writing his music, many of his quotations would have been readily recognized. And it is true, they would have been recognized by a particular kind of American audience, one that shared much of Ives's own type of background. To claim, however, that Ives would have wished all his "ideal listeners" to share the basic assumptions of his personal time, place, and culture seems at least problematic insofar as Ives's own aesthetic interests and goals are concerned. To claim further that late twentieth-century audiences should all immerse themselves in certain particularities of Ives's personal, local, and national heritage in order to understand his work would seem, in a way, to vastly underestimate both Ives's work and the potential audiences for it. I also find it difficult to believe that Ives would have wanted future listeners, from any background, to feel a need for cultural re-orientation or re-education in order to approach the substance of his work.

It seems clear that Ives's work aspires toward a universality that can render it, at least in some respects, independent of the circumstances of its creation. I feel that Ives's work deserves to endure only insofar as its fundamental meanings, and its expressive nuances, are capable of lifting themselves completely beyond the personal, local, and even national circumstances of their creation. I think Ives would have agreed with me, for he was interested in the personal, the local, even the national, only in terms of their ability to touch the universality of substance in art. He says as much in the epilogue to his *Essays Before A Sonata:* ". . . if local color, national color, any color, is a true pigment of the universal color, it is a divine quality, it is a part of substance in art—not of manner."

This suggests clearly that the agenda for those who wish to explore quotations in Ives should be to seek out the "universal color" in the local and national details of his material. In so doing, they will also lift their own work from local to potentially universal interest. On the other hand, I think Ives would have encouraged those who, from the distance of a late twentieth-century perspective, might choose rather to leap right toward the universal in his work, diving over the admittedly interesting aspects of personal, local, and national color, for the thrill of sudden immersion in the infinite—to stand, as Ives recommends, "unprotected from all the showers of the absolute!"

6

Juxtaposition and Sequence (III): Some Summarizing Works

This chapter will examine four remarkable works by Ives, in order to summarize and further explore those stylistic, formal, and conceptual approaches to his music that have been suggested thus far. The works are: the choral setting of *Psalm 90;* two songs, "On The Antipodes" and "General William Booth Enters Into Heaven"; and the orchestral movement "Decoration Day" from the *Holidays* Symphony. These pieces all give a feeling of artistic ambition and inclusiveness, as if Ives attempted to pour into each of them as much of his emotions, understanding, and compositional power as he possibly could.

Psalm 90, for chorus, organ, and bells, is one of Ives's last completed works. The published version is based on sources from 1923 and 1924. This piece reveals how conscious Ives had become of his own compositional methods toward the end of his creative career. Here, the brief instrumental introduction does not merely present material to be utilized later in the context of stylistically different sections. Instead, five stylistic "types" are specifically laid out in the introduction in a kind of musical shorthand—reduced to characteristic chord formations or brief progressions—and are identified by Ives's own labels in terms of the most significant textual associations each will accrue in the choral setting to follow. Furthermore, the order in which these "proto-styles" occur in the introduction directly forecasts the order of their presentation in the main body of the piece.

Example 6–1 shows the introduction to *Psalm 90*. In terms of Ives's actualization of the "proto-styles" in his ensuing choral setting, it is best to regard the final two measures of organ material here as a continuation of "Prayer and Humility," overlapping with the bell music that constitutes the distinctive essence of the "Rejoicing in Beauty and Work" style.

It is difficult to imagine a more schematic approach to musical style and form than that implicit in this introduction, or an approach that so closely links these musical essentials to the content and form of a text. Ives obviously appears here as a highly self-conscious artist, in contradistinction to the standard Ives mythology. The most interesting aspects of *Psalm 90* involve, in fact, not the execution of the stylistic and formal scheme outlined by the introduction, but rather the means employed by Ives to lend richness, subtlety, and complexity to what might seem an excessively preordained ground plan. Those characteristics of the form and of the text-setting that do not follow unambiguously from the introduction are those that create unpredictable and moving effects in this work. The effects are that much more striking because of their placement within a strong, clearly controlled overall form.

In many respects, then, *Psalm 90* reveals a kinship with the aesthetics of the Classical period, insofar as the major sources of interest and expressivity in the piece stem from the individuality with which the composer handles what would appear to be a fairly strict, imposed formal framework. Was Ives heading for a final, classical phase in his employment of stylistic diversity when his compositional career came to its unanticipated conclusion? It's a provocative, if unanswered and unanswerable, question.

Ives's setting of the first four verses of the psalm essentially presents the first four styles suggested by the introduction in sequence, one style for each verse. The appropriateness of this pattern, given Ives's labels for the different styles, is obvious from the text:

1. Lord, thou hast been our dwelling place from one generation to another.
2. Before the mountains were brought forth, or ever thou hadst formed the earth and the world, even from everlasting to everlasting, thou art God.

EXAMPLE 6–1. Ives, *Psalm 90*, mm. 1–5.

Copyright © 1960 Merion Music, Inc.
Used By Permission Of The Publisher.

3. Thou turnest man to destruction; and sayest, "Return, ye children of men."
4. For a thousand years in thy sight are but as yesterday when it is past, and as a watch in the night.

However, even from the first verse, unanticipated subtleties appear in Ives's setting enriching the musical life of the piece and suggesting further shadings of meaning in the text. It can be observed in Ex. 6–2 that the turning of man to destruction, first mentioned explicitly only in verse 3, is for Ives inevitable in the simple succession of generations, since the complex dissonant chord of "God's wrath against sin" suddenly appears to interrupt the serene, diatonic "Eternities" style as one generation brings forth *another*. The "wrath" chord type is repeated, on the further repetitions of the word "another," in wonderfully appropriate sequential transpositions upward. It is details like these that make the main body of *Psalm 90* much more than the straightforward execution of a simple plan proposed by its introduction.

The large central portion of *Psalm 90*, verses 5–13, is dominated by the style of "God's wrath against sin"; there are clear references also to the "Creation" and "Prayer and Humility" styles. Verses 9 and 12 stand out stylistically from the others. They are based upon whole-tone progressions, which could be viewed as very distant derivatives of the "Prayer and Humility" style (or as even more distant derivatives of the "God's wrath against sin" chord, which does contain some whole-tone elements). However, these passages sound in context much more like new styles, invented by Ives to underline the essential ideas of these verses, so crucial to the overall meaning and impact of the psalm:

9. For all our days are passed away in thy wrath: we spend our years as a tale that is told;
12. So teach us to number our days, that we may apply our hearts unto wisdom.

The final four verses of the psalm comprise the concluding section of the piece, which corresponds in scope to the opening section of four verses described earlier. Here, at last, the "Rejoicing in Beauty and Work" style, with its beautiful layered bell music, is heard, and prevails, essentially without interruption up to the end. Unlike the stylistically unstable opening, then, the conclusion of *Psalm 90* settles into one style, musically reflecting the sustained mood and hopefulness of the ending verses:

14. O satisfy us early with thy mercy; that we may rejoice and be glad all our days.

15. Make us glad according to the days wherein thou hast afflicted us, and the years wherein we have seen evil.
16. Let thy work appear unto thy servants, and thy glory unto their children.
17. And let the beauty of the Lord our God be upon us: and establish thou the work of our hands upon us; yea, the work of our hands establish thou it. Amen.

It is important to note, however, that the final style of *Psalm 90* is a layered style, and that its layers are composed of elements clearly related to the other styles heard individually in the piece. The music of the bells in the concluding section of *Psalm 90* is based entirely on the pitches heard in the bell parts of the introduction (see Ex. 6–1); the different repeated motives weave a harmonically ambiguous, polyrhythmic counterpoint around the diatonic, highly metrical organ and voice parts. The half step and augmented fifth intervals of Bell I come from the "Prayer and Humility" music; Bell III reiterates the notes of an augmented triad, also from the "Prayer and Humility" music; while Bell II outlines the notes used in the "Creation" chord, a grouping that also includes the notes of "The Eternities" chord. Bell IV simply states and restates the note C, which is present in the organ part throughout the piece, and which serves also as a central harmonic reference point for the choral parts throughout.

"God's wrath against sin" is absent from this layered construction (unless one chooses to regard the successive thirds in Bell III as an arcane reference to the intervallic construction of the "God's wrath" chord—I don't). This is fitting in music to accompany a prayer for reconciliation between God and humanity. The text for Verse 15 does make a point, however, of recalling "the days wherein thou hast afflicted us, and the years wherein we have seen evil." This *is* a reconciliation of wisdom, not of denial, and Ives obliges musically in the voices with a sudden variant of the "God's wrath" chord on the word "evil." Thus, some reference to each of the four major styles used earlier in the piece may be found in the concluding music of *Psalm 90*.

The ending of *Psalm 90* achieves a typically Ivesian richness and complexity within its unified, and unifying, effect. The goal of the spiritual journey described in the psalm is portrayed in musical terms not as a place totally set apart from the road travelled, but as a place of cumulative reconciliation in which different aspects of that road remain ever present. The

---

EXAMPLE 6–2. Ives, *Psalm 90*, mm. 6–15.

goal is the result of the journey, attained and maintained only through a total, unified awareness and acknowledgement of the journey itself. Ives is no religious escapist; his moving vision of salvation, which closes *Psalm 90*, is based not on denial or even on transcendence, as usually conceived, but on the complexity of knowledge (or "wisdom," to use the Psalmist's language) and of the ongoing "work of our hands."

In a closing gesture of a kind that has been shown to be typical of Ives, the soprano melody for the final verse of *Psalm 90* recalls directly the melodic line used for the opening verse. The texture is different at the end, of course, and not only because of the bells; the chorus, which sings in unison for most of verse 1, is here scored in four-part harmony evocative of traditional hymn-book style. There is also no reference to "God's wrath," as there is at the end of verse 1. Nevertheless, the ending retains some feeling of openness, due to the harmonic ambiguity of the bell parts, which sound particularly poignant against the hymn-book harmony of the chorus, and because the circling, directionless character of the bell music does not make possible any absolute impression of ending. Like the chorus, the bells fade "out of earshot," not because they have finished what they have to say— as the chorus has—but because their music by implication continues on forever, without any finish.

"On The Antipodes" is another late work by Ives based on schematic, self-conscious stylistic procedures. It was apparently completed in 1923, which makes it contemporaneous with *Psalm 90*. Like that work, it opens with an introduction setting forth material that will be systematically employed in the body of the piece. But in "On The Antipodes," the exact relationship of the introductory material to the text, meaning, and listener's aural experience of the whole is ambiguous, beneath the surface, and difficult to evaluate.

These complexities may well be intentional on Ives's part. The song ends, and climaxes, with a question, and certainly not a trivial one:

> Man! we ask you! Is Nature nothing but atomic cosmic cycles around the perennial antipodes?

(One responds not solely to the question, but perhaps even more to Ives's own memorable phrasing of it. The internal antipodean pairing of "atomic" and "cosmic" is particularly admirable.)

Since the piano introduction to this song bears a complicated, if fundamental, relationship to the main body of the piece, it will be best to consider the introduction after more obviously prominent features of the song as a whole have been discussed. Once the voice enters, "On The Antipodes" presents a succession of stylistic dichotomies, based on rapid alternations of tempo and texture, which illustrate in a very basic way the dualities presented by Ives's text:

Nature's relentless; Nature is kind.
Nature is Eternity; Nature's today!
Nature is geometry; Nature is mystery.
Nature's man's master; Nature's man's slave.

Example 6–3 shows that the successive contrasts sometimes focus basically on tempo, as in the first two phrases, and sometimes are expressed through tempo, texture, and articulation combined, as in the third and fourth phrases. Although significant changes occur from phrase to phrase in the pitch structures as well, these tend to be not so prominent, because of the generally dense texture and because of the consistent complexity of the pitch language itself.

Pitch contrast makes a more marked impression in the central pair of phrases in the song, where excessively genteel, banal C–major music is juxtaposed with ferociously dissonant music that is texturally and rhythmically disjunct to create a violent and wildly humorous effect (see Ex. 6–4). The juxtaposition of extremes here even extends, uncharacteristically for this piece, into the verbal realm; the mercilessly ironic grace note on "pansy" and the savage slide on "ain't" are telling musical responses to the poetic diction. Ives's special treatment of this central part of the song makes it an unequivocal high point from the standpoint of stylistic structure, presenting in an extreme form the work's characteristic behavior. Less violent juxtapositions surround this central part on either side.

The piano music accompanying "and, Sometimes 'it ain't'" in the climactic passage is a literal reiteration of the song's introductory sequence of chords, with all the note values halved. This creates a big formal articulation here from an additional standpoint. A varied, rhythmically augmented version of this same chord sequence is found at the conclusion of the song, where it produces a firm sense of overall symmetry in the song's structure as well as a seemingly inevitable return toward the point of departure. The sense of a *varied* return at the close is heightened by the totally new vocal line that articulates the "ultimate question" about nature; this contributes to the signature effect of an Ivesian open ending. (At the same time, the general sense of return at the ending is most appropriate, given the question in the text of whether everything in fact reduces to recurring cycles.)

We should now consider the material of the piano introduction, and its obviously important role in the total conception. It will be observed that the introductory sequence of chords begins with stacked fifths and progresses schematically through constructions using smaller and smaller intervals until, at midpoint, it arrives at a three-octave chromatic cluster of

EXAMPLE 6–3. Ives, "On The Antipodes," mm. 1–9.

From: Nineteen Songs.
Copyright © 1935 Merion Music, Inc.
Used By Permission Of The Publisher.

All notes are natural unless marked otherwise.
*The smaller notes in the voice part throughout are for lower voice, or voices, if there be a chorus.

EXAMPLE 6–4. Ives, "On The Antipodes," mm. 14–19.

From: Nineteen Songs.
Copyright © 1935 Merion Music, Inc.
Used By Permission Of The Publisher.

minor seconds, after which it reverses the process (see Ex. 6–3). This chord sequence as a whole encapsulates the basic pitch behavior of the entire work, with the exception of the sweet little passage in C major. Each chord from the introduction, in turn, engenders a brief phrase or two—occasionally only a single chord—in the piano part, built from its characteristic intervals. This process is interrupted only for the central passages shown in Ex. 6–4, after which it resumes from the point where it left off. When the entire sequence has run its course, we have arrived at the concluding question of the text, at which point the accompaniment presents the generative pitch structures, in varied form, consecutively one final time.

The introductory sequence of chords forms a nearly perfect pitch palindrome up to its final chord. Characteristically, the reiteration of this sequence, with diminished note values, in the central part of the piece does *not* occur precisely at the expected point. Like the generative palindrome itself, the central passages of Ex. 6–4 lie just this side of perfect symmetry. They do not occur right after the chord accompanying the phrase "Nature's man's slave," which is built from the palindrome's central minor seconds, but only after the *succeeding* piano phrase. Furthermore, the varied presentation of the introductory chord sequence at the end of the song also produces a slightly flawed palindrome.

Does the generative "flawed" chord sequence serve as a musical symbol, on some deep conceptual level, of the behavior and meaning of Ives's text, with its series of balanced antitheses leading up to a final unanswered question? Is the slightly askew overall design of the song yet another representation of the generally balanced, but ultimately ambiguous, character of Ives's conception? "On The Antipodes" seems to invite such provocative questions.

If the answers to these questions are far from straightforward in terms of a listener's actual experience of the piece, the difficulties may stem from further complexities and ambiguities that lie more on the musical surface. It is not possible to pinpoint a precise structural relationship between the generative chord sequence and many aspects of this song. Each chord type heard in the introduction does not generate a *distinct* stylistic area in the piece. Things go by too quickly; the pitch language is perhaps too complex throughout for ready differentiation of idioms, and in any case, single phrases of the song frequently use material engendered by more than one chord type. Furthermore, the vocal line itself bears no consistent relationship to the underlying chord structures, and the basic chord sequence is not obviously tied to any specific details of text treatment. (This is not to say that the song fails to express its text, but the meanings and contrasts of the text are expressed in terms of tempo, texture, rhythmic figures, and the general range and shaping of the vocal line much more than in terms relating to the generative chord sequence.)

Observers of Ives's music have noticed many types of patterns underlying the music of "On The Antipodes." There are "waves" of density and registral patterns, as well as pitch schemes. Those who have written on the piece all seem to agree that none of the "operating systems" relate in a simple, unambiguous way to the surface alternations of thesis and antithesis that give the piece its most obvious aural shape. What, then, is the significance of the underlying patterns in this song? And how do those patterns affect the success, or lack of success, of the song as a work of musical art?

There are obviously many possible responses to these questions. One might feel that the song is ultimately an unsuccessful work, that it lacks sufficient integration and realization of its compositional material into a coherent overall conception, resulting in a disharmony between style and substance. Or one might simply feel that the song is successful *despite* its arcane patterns and processes, because the surface is so effective in conveying mood and text. Perhaps the song could be viewed as successful because the underlying patterns operate on a level beneath consciousness, suggesting the "cycles" of nature along with their ambiguities and contradictions. Perhaps, for Ives, the issues posed by the song do not have nice and neat resolutions; both the surface and the hidden patterns, inconsistencies, and contradictions mirror this complexity in a way that results in a kind of "cosmic" harmony between style and substance.

> . . . if Ives never wrote but one song, he would have been a great composer. That's 'General William Booth Enters Into Heaven.' Now, I don't think anybody's said that before, have they? . . . It's a very great song. It's a song of genius, that's all.
> —*Carl Ruggles, in a 1969 interview*
>
> You won't get a heroic ride to Heaven on pretty little sounds!
> —*George Ives, as quoted by his son*

Any exploration of Ives's journey pieces should by all rights include at least some consideration of his overpowering setting of lines by Vachel Lindsay describing Salvation Army founder William Booth's ascent into heaven. Booth is accompanied on his journey by legions of urban unfortunates whom he is leading to salvation. At the crucial moment in the poem, Jesus appears, healing all the sick, lame, and blind members of "that blear review." Lindsay's lines are replete with sonic and specifically musical imagery—drums, banjos, trumpets, "big-voiced lassies" shrieking and singing—and must have tapped directly into the roots of Ives's rich experiences with church music and revival meetings, as well as into his own feelings as a deeply religious man. Ives's setting is a kind of extraordinary musical volcano that has impressed many observers as his greatest song.

"General William Booth Enters Into Heaven" explores a remarkable range of styles and feelings, creating an exceptionally broad musical canvas. Indeed, the song could well borrow a subtitle from William James: "The Varieties of Religious Experience." By turns solemn and ecstatic, muted and boisterous, dignified and even hysterical, it superbly summarizes Ives's technique of constructing an effective, wide-ranging, and ultimately unified whole from juxtapositions of stylistically diverse elements arranged in a form-producing sequence.

A step-by-step analysis of the piece seems unnecessary, if not sacrilegious, at this point in the study. I will attempt only an appreciation of a few individual and especially striking aspects.

Lindsay's poem uses as a refrain the words of the Salvation Army hymn "Are you washed in the blood of the Lamb?" Ives's compositional treatment of this refrain is fascinating in its richness. Certainly, he is not interested here in literal quotation for its own sake, because he doesn't quote the hymn melody traditionally associated with these words, but sets the words instead to a melodic quotation from a *different* hymn, Lowell Mason's "Foun-

93

tain.'' The text of the Mason hymn has a clear relationship to the imagery of the Salvation Army text, and so, for those who are knowledgeable concerning such matters, Ives achieves a double layer of association through his choice of borrowed material. But I don't think this is the essential point. I suspect that Ives chose the Mason tune primarily because it has such a strong, clear, immediately memorable *musical* shape, even for those unfamiliar with Protestant hymn traditions. With its emphasis on the notes of a simple major triad, it unequivocally evokes a traditional-sounding musical language whenever it appears. In context, this means of course that it sounds like a quotation, regardless of whether one specifically recognizes it as such. Even more importantly, this means also that it functions as an instantly recognizable stylistic reference point for the listener. Being paired in its recurrences with accompaniments differing in texture, rhythmic character, dissonance level, and tonal orientation (or lack of the same),

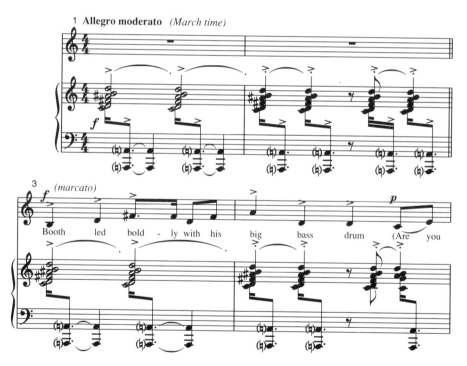

EXAMPLE 6–5. Ives, "General William Booth Enters Into Heaven," mm. 1–8; 75–80; 32–39.

From: Nineteen Songs.
Copyright © 1935 Merion Music, Inc.
Used By Permission Of The Publisher.

(continued)

Ives's musical refrain helps delineate with great clarity the differences in the styles of the various sections in which it occurs. This is illustrated by the set of excerpts shown in Ex. 6–5.

Observing the way in which Ives allows the refrain to function, it becomes apparent why he did not make the seemingly obvious choice of setting the refrain in a single, recurring musical style of its own and thus creating with

it a thematic and stylistic rondo. This would have made for an exact cor-
respondence between the form of the poem and that of the music, but the
inevitable consequence would have been a drastic loss in dramatic tension
and complexity, and a far too repetitive and predictable formal design. Ives

with a variant of the quoted tune:

(continued)

97

wants this musical journey to push *onward*, not double back on itself. Characteristically, he employs major stylistic recurrence only once in "Booth," and that is to make a large-scale unifying gesture in the last big section of the song, which returns to the style of the opening page of the piece without literal repetition.

A celebration of two delicious passages:

Example 6–6 occurs right in the middle of the song. First, the "big-voiced lassies," caught up in the utter frenzy of the moment, lose their bearings with an overexcited false start on "Are you?", which causes in turn an extra half-beat "hiccup" in the march rhythm. This is musical "naturalism" taken to hilarious extremes. Then, at the "Hallelujah," Ives reveals yet another use for his borrowed hymn refrain: altering the rhythmic pattern of its two highest notes creates a different rhythmic pattern suggesting Handel's famous "Hallelujah" chorus. (See the brackets in the example.) It will also be noticed that this "Hallelujah" passage brings further (shocked?) "hiccups" into the rhythm.

Example 6–7 shows the ending of the song. The refrain is heard for a final time, as if forming a coda to the piece. This *adagio* is set off by tempo, tonality, and style from the immediately preceding music, in which Ives

EXAMPLE 6–6. Ives, "General William Booth Enters Into Heaven," mm. 52–64.

From: Nineteen Songs.
Copyright © 1935 Merion Music, Inc.
Used By Permission Of The Publisher.

returned to the opening style of the song. (The opening style is seen in the very first hymn quotation illustrated previously in Ex. 6–5.) The voice here is securely in E major. Its first phrase is accompanied by indescribably rich harmonies which, while mixing triadic and whole-tone elements, clearly suggest tonic and subdominant functions in the key of E. Then, as

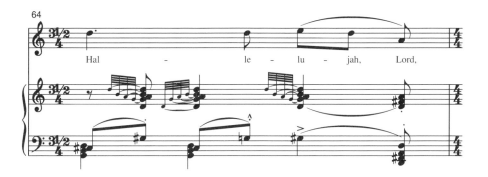

if picking up on this suggestion, the style of the accompaniment for the second, and final, vocal phrase changes into that of textbook diatonic harmony. This is a significant event, since musical style has not previously changed *during* a refrain in the song, and since triadic harmony has not been heard before in this pure a form. (The passages describing the entrance of Jesus come close to triadic harmony, but are full of "added sixths" which give the harmony at that point a sound distinctively different from what is heard here.) All of these factors suggest a summarizing gesture in the form of a concluding simplification of style, pointing clearly toward a cadence in E major. Booth's ragged band has been transformed and transfigured; the final resting place has been achieved; this journey does reach an ultimate goal. Why not then have a "real" ending, for once? Because the refrain is not an answer, but a *question*—and for the rest of us, left behind on the ground, a still unanswered one!

Ives brilliantly turns the refrain's question, which up to this point is probably perceived only as part of a beautifully depicted imaginary tableau, directly back on the listener, dissolving the illusion and leaving only bare, problematic reality: Are *you* washed in the blood of the Lamb? The sense of affectionate exaggeration, with which Ives consciously beguiles us throughout most of the song—and which is certainly present in Lindsay's poem—dissipates violently, as there are ultimately very serious issues at stake. Ives's ending forces us to entertain the idea that, in a spiritual sense, we—the privileged listeners—may not be that far removed at all from Booth's lepers, convicts, and loons (at whom we may have been laughing) *before* they were saved. These ones crossed over, but will we?

The connection with the unfortunate multitudes following Booth at the beginning of the piece is made, with a vengeance, by a whispered, fading, distorted return of the opening style—the style present immediately before the final refrain—and with which the song ends. As is so often the case, Ives achieves his startlingly open ending through compositional means that are extremely logical and formally satisfying from another point of view.

EXAMPLE 6–7. Ives, "General William Booth Enters Into Heaven," mm. 103–113.

From: Nineteen Songs.
Copyright © 1935 Merion Music, Inc.
Used By Permission Of The Publisher.

In retrospect, what seems like the coda—the final hymn refrain—is actually an interpolation, interrupting the prevailing final style of the piece. That this final style points us directly back toward the place of departure is only logical, given the question posed by the concluding line of text and, ironically, given rather conventional notions of musical unity. It is only our renegade desire to hear a "normal" cadence, a desire revealed by the composer to be illogical and inappropriate in this stylistic, formal, and spiritual context, that deceives us into believing for a moment that such a cadence might really provide an acceptable conclusion to this song. Ives here displays a virtually unparalleled understanding of the psychology of listening experience.

"Decoration Day," from Ives's *Holidays* Symphony, has proven to be one of the composer's more frequently performed large-scale instrumental works. It is also a work that has received much discussion in literature on Ives, in terms relating to the program provided for it by the composer, its use of quotation, and the aspects of Ives's psychological history that might be illuminated by it. "Decoration Day" suits the purposes of this study because it offers the opportunity to hear how clearly and remarkably Ives could apply his ideas about musical style and substance to a work of significant length—which achieves its communication without a text, and without the listener needing any knowledge of program, quotation, or the composer's psychological history.

Ives's title suggests directly that this piece is about remembrance. (The holiday Decoration Day is now called Memorial Day.) The nature of his music in this piece tells us that a physical journey is being evoked. One could hardly imagine a more quintessentially Ivesian mixture of concerns—journey and memory—and "Decoration Day" is thus in many respects an ideal summarizing work.

Despite its duration of more than eight minutes, the form of "Decoration Day" can readily be apprehended, and that form is created by clear alterations in style. Table 6–1 identifies the three basic styles that are evident in the work, and the sectional form created by their employment. Also included are timing indications, which pinpoint the beginnings of the indicated sections on two of the best-known recordings of this work; these timings will facilitate integration of the other information in the table directly into the listening experience.

The brief introduction to "Decoration Day" is clearly analogous in type and function to the piano introductions found in "Ann Street" and "Tom Sails Away." It puts forward, in a nonliteral fashion, stylistic elements that will be utilized more systematically later on in the piece. Most obviously, this introduction hints at the main melodies of Sections 1 and 2, and presents drum taps that foreshadow the slow, steady march rhythm of Section 2.

It will readily be noticed that Sections 1 through 3 form a progression from slow, sparsely textured, dissonant, irregularly metered music to a conventional-sounding, fast-moving, fully scored march. In contrast to the deliberately fragmented impressions created in Section 1, Section 3 presents a complete march tune. (It is Reeves's *Second Regiment Connecticut March*, of which Ives was particularly fond.) The march has traditionally balanced phrases and even a clear internal form, consisting of: two statements of the main tune; two statements of a short "bridge," the second of which is varied and shortened by one measure; and a brief concluding figure, also heard twice, derived from the main tune. Section 2 represents a kind of stylistic midpoint between Sections 1 and 3, as the chart of styles shows.

A typically Ivesian source of unity among the stylistic sections of "Decoration Day" is the sharing of particular intervallic constructions. The most prominent motive connected with style "A," and the motive first heard in Section 1, is a little five-note figure of very limited range, which oscillates around a central pitch. A similar "turning" motive forms part of the sustained melody heard in Section 2, and an analogous motive also plays a role in the march tune of Section 3. While these connections are not the

104

TABLE 6–1

"Decoration Day": Basic Styles and Sections

THE STYLES

Style	Melody	Harmony	Rhythm	Orchestration	Other
"A"	Brief motives, like tune fragments, developed in disjunct fashion.	Relatively dissonant; no stable sense of pitch center.	Slow-moving; improvisatory effect due to constant meter changes.	Basically sparse; strings and solo winds are featured.	Very soft dynamic level, rising occasionally louder.
"B"	Emergence of a continuous, flowing line; diatonic intervals emphasized.	Relatively more consonant; triadic constructions, but still no stable center.	Slow, steady pulse; stable 4/4 meter prevails.	Fuller winds and strings; more sustained texture; bells in background.	Still soft; very stable dynamic level throughout.
"C"	Jaunty, traditional march tune in major key.	"Common practice" chord progressions in major key; traditional alignment of harmony with melody.	Fast-moving, conventional 6/8 meter.	Full orchestra, with brass and percussion especially emphasized.	Very loud dynamic level prevails.

THE SECTIONS

Section	Style Used	Starting Time: Bernstein*	Starting Time: Tilson Thomas†
INTRODUCTION	[Elements of A & B]	0:01	0:01
[Brief silence		0:24	0:29]
SECTION 1	A	0:27	0:32
[Brief silence		3:36	3:53]
TRANSITION	[Elements of A & B]	3:37	3:55
SECTION 2	B	4:39	5:18
TRANSITION	[Anticipates and leads into C]	6:08	7:12
SECTION 3	C (with additional layered elements)	7:02	8:17
"CODA"	A (briefly recalled)	7:57	9:14
[End		8:36	9:56]

* Leonard Bernstein conducting the New York Philharmonic, CBS cassette MPT-39556 (includes the complete *Holidays* Symphony)
† Michael Tilson Thomas conducting the Chicago Symphony Orchestra and Chorus, CBS cassette MT-42381 or CBS compact disc MK-42381 (includes the complete *Holidays* Symphony)

most prominent feature of the piece, they help to create an integral impression, if only on a subconscious level.

As in "Walking" and "The Things Our Fathers Loved," there are areas of stylistic transition in "Decoration Day." The transition between Sections 1 and 2 establishes, for the first time in the piece, a stable meter, the 4/4 meter that will characterize Section 2. A regular, slow march pulse is clearly delineated at the start of this transition, becomes momentarily obscured, and is then re-established just before the entrance of the sustained melody whose arrival announces the formal beginning of Section 2. Continuity with Section 1 is assured through the persistence of the most important melodic motive of that section—the little oscillating figure identified previously—into the opening measures of the transition.

The transition between Sections 2 and 3 introduces a diatonic tune played by an offstage trumpet; built on an arpeggiated major triad, the tune prefigures the melodic and harmonic basis of the forthcoming style "C." (The tune, of course, is "Taps.") This transition also maintains a relationship with Section 2 through the continuing sound of the bells and the persistence of a somewhat complex harmonic idiom, created by melodically and harmonically independent lines (of which the bells are one element) heard against the trumpet tune. Toward the end of the transition, a vigorous crescendo and accelerando, complete with percussive chords that are reminiscent of passages in "General William Booth Enters Into Heaven," leads directly into Section 3.

Up to the end of Section 3, "Decoration Day" seems to be moving gradually toward a simpler style. Section 3 actually offers a conventional ending in this simpler style, only to have the complex and unconventional opening style of the work return afterward—to have the "last word" in a way suggesting an obvious analogy to the ending passages of "General William Booth Enters Into Heaven." The effect of this in "Decoration Day" is as brilliantly disorienting as it is in the song, if not more. Ives deliberately sets the novel but forceful logic of his stylistically rounded ending against the familiar impact of a huge C–major cadence, inviting the listener to acknowledge that, for all its traditional weight as a big, final, "happy" ending gesture, the C–major cadence is *not* the truly appropriate conclusion for "Decoration Day."

Apart from the straightforward formal logic, which suggests that an opening style should return to end a work, Ives provides additional reasons for the listener to feel that Section 3 cannot really conclude the piece. Although I have referred to the sense of gradual stylistic progression that informs "Decoration Day," and to Section 2 as a kind of stylistic midpoint in the piece, it cannot be denied that these aspects are experienced more as abstract conceptualizations than as part of the actual listening experience. This is because Section 3, its many relationships to the preceding music notwithstanding, actually comes across as an unanticipated and virtually shattering contrast to all that has preceded it.

It is another case of Ives choosing deliberately to stress the compositional effects of abruptness and apparent incongruity over those that might better point up connectedness. The sudden explosion in the orchestration, dynamic level, and tempo at the start of Section 3 eclipses everything else, at least for the moment. In retrospect, we are compelled to realize and admire the obviously studied restraint Ives has exercised in his use of the orchestra up to this point, and how prevailingly slow and soft he has kept the music, so that Section 3 will achieve its desired effect. That effect is a strange mixture of intense release and a feeling of imbalance.

A look at Ives's score reveals some further anomalies about Section 3. While the vivacious C–major march is in progress, softer musical effects, which fail to correspond to the basic style, are present. The bell music continues from Section 2 and the transition, providing an incongruous "layer" of music throughout Section 3 that coexists with, but does not interact with, the march. There are also many other seemingly "inappropriate" details, including "off-key" notes in several instruments before and at the final C–major cadence. Unfortunately, most of these inspired touches are virtually inaudible in the recorded performances of "Decoration Day," which leaves us with several unanswered questions. Could a determined conductor successfully bring these effects out better? Would it require a live performance to make them clearly audible? Did Ives simply miscalculate the orchestral balances in this section, or did he perhaps wish for these special details to be heard and experienced on a subconscious level, if such a thing is possible? In any case, Ives must have intended these details to subtly render Section 3 less conclusive and even further off-balance.

A glance at the durations of the three main stylistic sections in "Decoration Day" shows that each of these sections is significantly shorter than the preceding one. As the music gathers rhythmic momentum, its formal units become progressively more concise in terms of real time, until we arrive at the brief, powerful juggernaut that is Section 3. The effect is perhaps something like that of foreshortening in the visual arts; it certainly seems to have something to do with suggesting spatial "perspective," since the music gives the clear illusion of coming closer to us, and more into focus, as it goes along. This argument suggests two further rationales to justify the final return to style "A." One could say that the "coda" continues and rounds off the process just described. It is shorter than any of the preceding stylistic sections, while it concludes and "resolves" the shortening process by pairing the briefest duration and the style originally associated with the formal unit of *longest* duration. Or, one might claim that the abrupt and violent intensity of Section 3 creates a need to step back "outside" the process entirely, to gain an overview of the whole; such a "perspective" is beautifully provided by the fleeting return of the style associated with the first, the longest, and the most leisurely of all the sections.

The "coda" recalling style "A" is already in progress when we start to hear it, because its opening notes are attacked softly by a few instruments *before* the big chord that ends Section 3 has finished sounding. This is a lovely and poignant effect, which emerges with particular clarity in the performance conducted by Michael Tilson Thomas. It represents an instance of the kind of overlapping of styles that was encountered previously in "Walking." After recalling the opening measures of Section 1, the "coda" veers off into a kind of distorted "Amen" cadence, concluding the work with this gentle, startlingly effective alternative to the boisterous C–major ending of Section 3.

"Coda" is admittedly not a good term for an ending section which, however brief, bears as much structural and expressive importance as the ending section of "Decoration Day," but I'm not sure what else to call it. If we accept "coda," then this ending of "Decoration Day" is a coda in the same sense that the section in the first movement of Beethoven's "Eroica" Symphony which follows the recapitulation is a coda—all 135 measures of it!

And what complex of emotions is expressed by the ending of "Decoration Day," with its convincing and telling rejection of the rousing military march as an appropriate conclusion for the experiences explored in the work? Ives's formal structuring of the piece is beautifully calculated to expose both the great virtues and the great limitations of the kind of music represented by Section 3. The burst of welcome familiarity and stylistic simplicity in Section 3 is indeed exhilarating—but it's *too* exhilarating, too *simplistically* exhilarating to provide a true culmination for the intense, complicated emotions and experiences suggested by the earlier sections of the work. The experiences of Sections 1 and 2 are too rich and ambiguous to find adequate resolution in Section 3. Style "C" may be the strictly linear goal of a stylistic progression toward simplicity but, instead of synthesizing and resolving the earlier music, it makes us momentarily *forget* that music in a rush of excitement. The great shock, and meaning, of the coda is that it forces upon us the realization that we had forgotten all about that earlier music. By presenting some of it again, the coda reminds us how profoundly moving and how important that music was, and still is. If anything, the emotional pull of the opening music of Section 1 is heightened and made more urgent when it reappears in this context.

Ives's music can communicate all this, and much more. It needs to be stressed that the music can communicate without a program, and regardless of whether we recognize its quotations, or possess any knowledge of the composer's cultural background or psychological history. This is true simply because Ives is first and foremost a *composer*—he is not primarily a story-teller, tune anthologist, cultural or psychological artifact, or curiosity.

Once we can accept this we can turn to Ives's program, and to the interpretations and commentary of scholars, for an enrichment of our basic *musical* experience. Ives's own program spells out the details of gathering flowers, solemnly parading to the cemetery, decorating the graves of the Civil War dead, and marching back to town. When we realize that this piece is, among other things, a meditation about death, the complexity of much of its music becomes more accessible, and in particular, the meaning of its ending becomes that much more pointed. We understand in a more specific and urgent way why the big military march is used, and why its aggressive but formulaic expression of "patriotism" cannot be allowed to conclude the piece. The meaning is intensified, but only because the basic meaning was implicit to begin with in the behavior of the music. Ives's words function as a lovely, poetic adjunct to his music, not as a causal explanation for it.

The other three movements of the *Holidays* Symphony are as rewarding as "Decoration Day." Like "Decoration Day," they all explore aspects of relatively familiar and unfamiliar styles, arranged in provocative sequences and juxtapositions. Although each movement was composed separately, expressive larger patterns and relationships certainly emerge from the grouping and specific arrangement of the four together. It is left to the reader to explore how Ives creates even larger stylistic structures of re-markable import and importance when he fashions a multimovement epic like *Holidays*.

Performance, Professionalism, and Amateurs

The references to aspects of performance, which arose during the preceding discussion of "Decoration Day," encourage a brief digression on the matter of performing Ives's music. Why do Ives's scores tend to *look* so difficult? Are some of them really as "impossible" to perform as they appear to be?

It is true that the appearance of many Ives scores (not all of them, however) seems to invite, if not require, the ministration of highly–trained professional musicians to decipher them accurately. Alas, although pro-fessional musicians are well trained to read the literal notes and rhythms in such scores, their training too often acts to discourage the kind of per-formance approach that might truly decipher and convey Ives's *aesthetic* intentions. In fact, Ives had a far greater love for the strong amateur music-making he heard during his formative years than he did for most of the professional music-making—and music-makers—he encountered throughout his life. The spirit of the best amateur music-making informs much of Ives's mature work as a composer, and it is necessary to understand this spirit thoroughly and sympathetically in order to perform Ives's work idiomatically.

Ives's music receives too many well-meaning, but stilted and artificial-sounding, professional performances that lack the necessary Ivesian spontaneity of gesture and effect. Ives would surely have preferred sincere, rough-and-ready amateur attempts at performing his scores to pompously correct, professional ones. He understood, perhaps better than anyone else ever has, that amateur music-making can be as inspiring and as wonderful as any music-making. "You won't get a heroic ride to Heaven on pretty little sounds," and you can't sing "General William Booth Enters Into Heaven" like a traditional *lieder* singer, either.

Ironically, although Ives rejected a professional career in music, very few of his characteristic mature compositions can actually be performed by typical amateurs. As a composer, Ives was not, and could never be, a typical "amateur," for the simple reason that, professional or not, he was a musical genius. So he left music that seems to address neither typical amateur performers nor typical professional performers—which is the source of most of the difficulty. The ideal Ives performance would actually be a synthesis of professional and amateur virtues. It would combine the kind of assurance and know-how that is characteristic of the truest, least self-conscious professionalism with the sense of spontaneous exuberance and enthusiasm associated with the best amateur musicianship. And that's a tall order!

The connection that Ives's music seeks to make with the sounds and spirit of amateur performance helps explain why his music at times looks so odd. That is to say, he was inspired by kinds of musical experiences that often did not proceed from traditional notation, or that just as often ignored it. The sound experiences Ives imagined as a composer were not necessarily "difficult" inherently, or even unduly complex. It is rather that our notational system was not designed to deal gracefully with many of these sound experiences. Ives's scores may be seen as the written record of his struggles to fit his spontaneous aural imagination somehow into the framework of a rather unsympathetic, intransigent system of documentation. This is why performers of his music require unusual imagination even more than specific technical skills. In fact, the more difficult or even "impossible" Ives's notation may appear in a given instance, the more he may be inviting the performer to *free* himself from the notation at that point. Ives's "impossibilities" should not discourage adventurous amateurs from attempting to play his music; rather, they should encourage professional performers of his music to behave more like idealized, inspired, intrepid amateurs.

The ideas just put forward can be defended and clarified by offering three specific illustrations of them: a personal performance experience; an account of Ives's experience with a performance; and Ives's actual instructions on a score.

My personal experience took place a few years ago when I was preparing a recital with a talented student singer who asked me to accompany her in a performance of "General William Booth Enters Into Heaven." I accepted the offer with excitement, but also with some hesitation and anxiety. I knew that, as an amateur pianist, I would never be able to play that "impossible" piece correctly. Confronted with six- and seven-note chords in the right hand that had to be struck in quick succession, I soon discovered that if I concentrated on the most "impossible" aspect, that of having my thumb always play the correct two (or three!) notes in each chord, I would hopelessly erode the tempo and lose the desired tone quality, not to mention the needed spontaneity, of the performance. (As frequently as not, I'd also lose most of the other notes in the chords.) Eventually, however, I came to understand that Ives's huge "piano-drum" chords were a way of calling not for every specific indicated pitch, but for a kind of aggressive, wide-handed approach to the keyboard that would assure the *quality* of musical experience he wanted. Once I adopted that approach, the appropriate musical quality was obtained—with results no less "accurate" than those produced by an excessive concentration on the "right" notes. Thus Ives gave me a profound "piano lesson" I have not forgotten.

One of the few times Ives himself attended a professional performance of any of his works was when he heard Nicolas Slonimsky conduct *Three Places in New England* in 1931. As the Cowells tell it, the performance was enthusiastic but "somewhat scrambling." Ives, however, expressed delight rather than outrage at the ragged quality, and apparently told Slonimsky afterward that it was "Just like a town meeting—every man for himself. Wonderful how it came out!"

This last anecdote illustrates a fascinating paradox relating to American cultural history and to the emerging character of Ives's music in performance. While many traditions of American amateur music-making, which Ives loved, are perhaps becoming like endangered species in an increasingly urbanized society, where the production of music is becoming more of a technological phenomenon than a shared community activity, Ives's scores help perpetuate the spirit of those American amateur traditions. Through Ives's music, professionals, and the most intrepid amateurs, can still recapture that spirit—if they interpret the scores appropriately. Whether Ives consciously saw it this way, and fashioned his scores deliberately as a means to preserve the spirit of his beloved traditions in a radically changing society, I don't know, but he couldn't have done a better or a more thorough job of it.

To conclude, let us look at the score of an Ives song, which even goes so far as to tell the performer in one critical passage to forget about the deliberately "impossible" actual notes, and just play *something* in time. Example 6–8 shows the climactic portion of Ives's "cowboy" song, "Charlie Rutlage," the greatest country-and-western number never to be performed at the Grand Ole Opry.

This song is about performance as much as anything else. It begins in a more or less traditional style, with the voice singing a diatonic tune and the piano accompanying with octaves and triads in a boom-chick "western" pattern. As the tale of Charlie's misfortune on the roundup unfolds, the voice slips from singing into rhythmized speech; Ives indicates rhythmic values but no pitches for the singer, as the narrator presumably becomes too excited to sing and instead speaks directly to the auditors. Meanwhile, the piano part becomes more and more agitated and dissonant. The tonality is lost, and sevenths and ninths are added to the chords. When Charlie falls and his horse falls on him, the piano loses all specific pitch focus, as may be seen in the example. Here, "the time, of course, is the main point." After the noise of the piano's tone clusters, the singer recollects himself and is able to sing again, and the piano finds its way progressively back from dissonant chords to the opening triads.

At specific points in "Charlie Rutlage," Ives makes explicit with what his performers do and don't need to concern themselves. In effect, he uses this aspect of compositional control (or decontrol) as a way of manipulating style and of creating form through this manipulation of style. Although the song is an extreme, and an extremely effective, example of this procedure, "Charlie Rutlage" offers clear implications for the interpretation of Ives's intentions elsewhere—especially in those works based similarly on vernacular styles.

There are many Ives pieces that make specific allowances for choice by performers, offering alternative versions of certain passages, suggestions for alternative instrumentation, and so forth. In the area of rhythm alone, one could point to the significant number of songs without any bar–line notation—or with only occasional bar lines—and to the large quantity of unbarred piano music Ives produced. Such instances are numerous enough to encourage analogous performer freedoms in many works that do not explicitly call for them. Of course, there are also many Ives works where there's precise notation for every aspect of what he wanted, which is sufficient to indicate that his wishes must be unequivocally respected in these cases. We have seen some examples of this in "The Things Our Fathers Loved." Characteristically, the most specific attention to detail is

*In these measures, the notes are indicated only approximately; the time of course, is the main point.

EXAMPLE 6–8. Ives, "Charlie Rutlage," mm. 33–45.

often found in those pieces where an open, relatively spare texture and an absence of pitch and rhythmic "difficulties" make it easily possible for Ives's notation to be actualized by performers and heard by listeners. The composer's stylistic spectrum clearly embraces a wealth of attitudes toward performance, and consequently offers a highly stimulating range of possibilities—and impossibilities!—to the performer.

7

Layering

Occasional instances of Ives's layering of styles upon one another have already been encountered in the course of examining works that take their form from the juxtaposition and sequence of styles. Ives's layering actually encompasses two distinct techniques. One is the creation of new *composite* styles from conceptually separable elements; this was seen in *Over The Pavements,* in the bitonal interludes of the *Variations on "America,"* and in the concluding section of *Psalm 90.* In such cases, the resulting music is experienced by the listener in terms of a single, albeit complex, stylistic unit. In the other form of layering, the emphasis is on multiplicity rather than combination, as the listener experiences the coexistence of two or more independent stylistic planes. Momentary instances of this type of layering have been noted in "Walking" and in "Decoration Day," at points where the styles of two adjacent sections overlap. However, Ives could also build entire pieces from this second kind of layering, pieces in which differing styles exist and develop not in turn, but simultaneously.

Such layering of stylistically independent musics has profound implications, and arguably requires even a greater adjustment on the listener's part than Ives's utilization of varying styles in sequence. When styles are presented side by side, they can be seen as analogous in certain ways to thematic areas in more traditional compositions. When styles are superimposed, obviously no such analogy is possible; what we have then is perhaps a kind of counterpoint, though the relationship to any traditional notion of counterpoint seems strained indeed. Those Ives pieces that layer independent styles seem designed to emphasize the sense of stylistic separation throughout, and not to point toward any conventional resolution or balancing of the separate elements. These works speak with particular forcefulness to life's irresolutions and incongruities, to those coexisting aspects of existence that do not interact with—sometimes, do not even acknowledge—one another.

For obvious reasons, stylistic superimposition functions most effectively where there are a number of performers and types of musical timbre available. In such instances, each stylistic layer can project the maximum individual identity and independence. The best-known example of this type of layering, *The Unanswered Question*, presents three stylistic streams: one played by a group of string instruments, one played by a solo trumpet, and one played by four flutes. In *Central Park in the Dark*, another celebrated piece, a string body presents one stylistic layer while winds, brass, percussion instruments, and piano superimpose another. In the massive scherzo of the Fourth Symphony, different sections and subsections of an enormous orchestra delineate a complex of stylistic layers.

The song medium is not an obvious choice for this kind of layering; however, Ives wrote one major song that beautifully exemplifies it: "The Housatonic at Stockbridge." It is not surprising that this song was derived directly from an orchestral piece (of the same name, the third movement of *Three Places in New England*). The opening pages of the song are shown in Ex. 7–1.

The clear separation of stylistic layers in the piano part at the outset of the piece is achieved through dynamic, harmonic, and rhythmic means. As may be seen in the example, there is even a visual component to the stylistic separation, as the right-hand part is printed with smaller note heads than the left-hand part. The left hand presents—despite Ives's rather inconsistent spelling of pitches—a diatonic melody in C$^\sharp$ major, which moves basically in slow half-note motion over a firm pedal point on C$^\sharp$ and G$^\sharp$. (This melody anticipates that of the voice; in mm. 3 and 4, the motive that will be heard on "dreamy realm" is presented literally in long note-values.) Over the left-hand material, at what Ives directs in his note to be a "scarcely audible" dynamic level, the right-hand part presents a steady stream of eighth notes, basically on the white keys, and phrased in rhythmic groupings independent of the clear duple meter suggested by the left-hand music. While the music of the lower part is characterized, throughout the piano introduction and into the body of the song, by consistent and unambiguous tonality and rhythmic character, the upper part is already introducing fresh harmonic and rhythmic developments into its style by the third measure. However, the upper part remains obviously patterned enough to retain a

NOTE:- The small notes in the right hand may be omitted, but if played should be scarcely audible. This song was originally written as a movement in a set of pieces for orchestra, in which it was intended that the upper strings, muted, be listened to separately or sub-conciously, as a kind of distant background of mists seen through the trees or over a river valley, their parts bearing little or no relation to the tonality, etc. of the tune. It is difficult to reproduce this effect with piano

EXAMPLE 7–1. Ives, "The Housatonic at Stockbridge," mm. 1–19.

(continued)

firm sense of style, a style thoroughly incongruous with that of the other layer in the texture. Of course, the two styles are clearly separated by register, and consequently by tone color, as well.

A glance at the very beginning of the orchestral score for "The Housatonic at Stockbridge," Ex. 7–2, reveals the richness and complexity of Ives's

EXAMPLE 7–2. Ives, "The Housatonic at Stockbridge," from *Three Places in New England*, mm. 1–4.

Copyright © 1935 Mercury Music Corporation.
Used By Permission Of The Publisher.

(continued)

119

original conception. It will be noticed that the upper string music here is much more elaborate than in Ives's piano reduction; the latter preserves only the second and third violin parts, omitting the chromatic haze woven above, around, and under these parts by Violins I and IV, and by the violas. Indeed, in the orchestral version, this upper layer is *itself* a layered style, consisting of both diatonic and chromatic elements, and providing a good example of a composite style that is, in context, perceived as a unit. The extremely soft dynamics and muted sonority of this upper string music, along with the constant crisscrossing of its individual lines, obscure the separate elements and create a gentle, swirling but uniform, wash of color. This forms a consistent and atmospheric backdrop for the more prominent layer, which is heard clearly beneath it in the lower strings, the left hand of the orchestral piano, and the bassoon.

The sense of harmonic, rhythmic, and textural separation between the two stylistic layers in the orchestral version of "The Housatonic at Stockbridge" is much more profound than in the version for voice and piano. Even Ives acknowledges, in his note on the first page of the song's score, how difficult it is to achieve anything even resembling the extraordinary orchestral effects on the keyboard alone. Still, as one who has tried, I can report that it is well worth attempting to do so. To omit the right-hand piano part in a performance of the song—a choice Ives rather uncharacteristically permits in his note to the performer—would be to lose the layered quality entirely, and along with it all of the most distinguishing qualities of this work.

When the voice enters in the song, it in effect joins the stylistic layer being presented by the left hand of the piano. Melodically, harmonically, and rhythmically, the vocal line and the lower piano part constitute one complex unit, from which the upper piano part remains independent.

The two layered styles in "The Housatonic at Stockbridge" are subtly connected through their sharing of certain intervallic patterns, as is so often the case with different styles Ives may use within a single piece. (This particular aspect emerges with particular clarity in the song, since pitch structures in the upper layer emerge clearly in the relatively uncrowded texture.) Intervals of thirds, especially major thirds, stand out in the music of both layers. In the upper layer, thirds are used obviously and continuously as a vertical element, while the emerging melody in the lower layer repeatedly emphasizes the F♯ or E♯ major third of its prevailing C♯ major harmony. When the voice enters, it articulates the major third as a melodic motive, on "Contented river," and this becomes the central motive for the entire vocal line (and for the main melody in the orchestral version).

Example 7–1 shows that the vocal line does not simply reinforce an already present stylistic layer in the music; it adds enormously to that layer's development. Accepting the tonal center, melodic suggestions, and rhythmic orientation of the lower stylistic layer, the vocal melody soon nudges that layer into richer melodic, harmonic, and even rhythmic realms. This comes as a gradual and logical development, not as a disruption of style. By the end of the second page of score, the voice has led its layer into some melodic and chordal pitches that lie outside the circumscribed area of purely diatonic C♯ major harmony, and into an expressive 5/4 alteration in the prevailing meter as the eye "wanders" with the river.

It will also be noticed that during these first two pages of the song, Ives occasionally allows some isolated details in the upper stylistic layer to emerge out of the background into the visual foreground of his score. This hints at compositional manipulation of the "spatial" foreground-background relationship between the two layers, something that will come to play an increasingly essential role later on in this piece. Thus, development does not occur only on the level of the individual stylistic layer; more significantly, the piece comes to be about the "distance" between the layers themselves. It is because he establishes his layers so firmly in the piano introduction that Ives can work with them in the body of the song to affect and illuminate its emerging meaning.

On a musical level, that meaning has to do with the inherent incongruity between one style, which is defined by a very specific tonal and metrical character, and another style not defined by any specific tonal or metrical character. This is much more than a disjunction between two tonalities or two rhythmic systems. What Ives presents in "The Housatonic at Stockbridge" are two quite different approaches to musical construction and coherence. In the preceding chapters of this study, we have seen how Ives often juxtaposes such different approaches within a single work, and have examined ways of discovering meaning in these juxtapositions. But how is the listener to understand the *simultaneous* coexistence of apparently opposing styles?

The explicit foreground-background relationship between the styles, which is established by Ives at the outset of "The Housatonic at Stockbridge," suggests one way of interpreting the aural message. The upper layer may be heard as a kind of undifferentiated musical mass, out of which the clearly delimited style of the lower layer may be heard to "emerge"—just as, following the suggested imagery of Ives's note, the view of a river may emerge out of a background of "mists." An anomaly is that the upper layer remains present (along with the "mists"), "clouding" the view and rendering it subtly ambiguous. (Later on in the poem, the river is accused of being "overshy": "Hast thou a thought to hide from field and town?") This effect is much more marked in the orchestral version, but it will not be absent from a sensitive performance of the song. The persistent backdrop provided by the upper layer can seem rather anonymous and soothing. But it may become an aural irritant after awhile, as the ear strains to latch on to pitches in the background that "belong" to the language of the foreground music, only to find that they are passing happenstances in the style of the upper layer, and point toward no real resolution of the dichotomy.

One interpretation that probably would *not* occur to most listeners during the opening portion of the song, especially given the foreground-background relationship of styles at the outset, is that the more conventional, tonal style could be a foil to the *other* style in a developing dramatic conception. Most of us, after all, lean toward the more familiar. I suspect this is exactly what Ives has been counting on when, in the remarkable climax of "The Housatonic at Stockbridge," he violently alters the interrelationship of his stylistic layers and allows chromatic, dissonant, rhythmically unpredictable music to take over the piece. In the score to the song, Ives does a wonderful job of showing how the style of the upper layer emerges out of the background (see Ex. 7–3). By the end of the example, this style dominates the foreground; above and beyond that, there is no longer any audible background into which the other style can recede. The voice here loses all sense of tonal bearings, as it joins with the accompaniment in a thickly-textured, but unified, style that has completely assumed the basic characteristics previously associated with the upper, "background" layer. The more traditional style has simply been swept away by the sudden headlong rush of the river, but more importantly, of the thoughts inspired by the river.

By this point, Ives seems forcibly to be suggesting that interpretation of his song's meaning should proceed onto a different plane entirely. Suddenly, the dynamic potential of the original background layer is revealed. No longer an amorphous backdrop or an anomalous distraction, it is shown to be a source of enormous musical energy and expressivity, which profoundly enriches the song's expressive palette. This climactic section builds right up to the end of the poem, where the poet/singer urges the river, "Let me tomorrow thy companion be,/By fall and shallow to the adventurous sea!"

However, this is not the end of the story musically. The sudden explosion of musical power creates the sense of a formal imbalance that demands restoration. The complex, atonal style can serve many previously unsuspected functions, but satisfactorily concluding the piece is not one of them. Ives is obliged to add a coda (Ex. 7–4).

When the damper pedal comes off the huge chord on "sea," we find already layered "underneath" it the soft initial chord of Ives's coda; the overlapping effect is beautifully captured when Ives's careful pedal instructions are followed exactly. The coda is a brief reminiscence of the song's more traditional style, which was so effectively "submerged" by the other style as the song rushed to its climax. On one level, the coda of "The Housatonic at Stockbridge" can be experienced simply and meaningfully, as an awestruck catch-breath at the power revealed at the song's climax. But we are also made to understand here that the dissonant, disjunct style, far from rendering the more traditional style irrelevant or inexpressive, has in fact created a *need*, which the return of that style perfectly satisfies. In

EXAMPLE 7–3. Ives, "The Housatonic at Stockbridge," mm. 29–33.

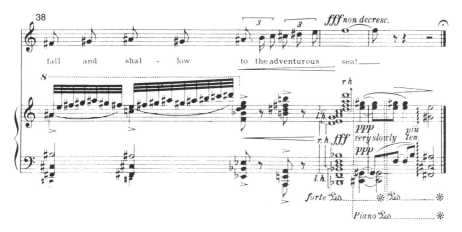

EXAMPLE 7–4. Ives, "The Housatonic at Stockbridge," mm. 38–40.

Copyright © 1954 by Peer International Corporation.
Used by Permission.

separation, the two styles clearly reveal their individual expressive potentialities, but they are also made to reveal that they need each other. In the
afterglow of this ending, the listener may retrospectively come to view the
stylistic layering that characterizes most of "The Housatonic at Stockbridge"
as representing not an anomalous situation, but rather a condition of equi-
librium, wherein stylistic (and perhaps natural) forces and potentialities
coexist in a state of mutual balance.

The ending of "The Housatonic at Stockbridge" suggests a kind of inverse
analogy to the ending of "Decoration Day." In the former piece, a sudden
explosion of intense, unrelievedly complex music necessitates a return to
a "simpler" style; in the latter, an explosion of abrupt "simplicity" triggers
a return to a more subtle, complicated idiom. In both works, relationships
between very unlike musical styles, and our experiences of them, are put
forward compositionally in unprecedented and challenging ways. Each
piece also provides a marvelous illustration of one of Ives's most memorable
musings about the course of stylistic evolution in music: ". . . why tonality
as such should be thrown out for good, I can't see. Why it should be always
present, I can't see."

What Ives provides in the coda to "The Housatonic at Stockbridge" is
not a literal recurrence. The traditional style heard earlier in the song is
subtly altered here to yield further expressive potential, just as the other
style of the piece is expanded and developed to serve new purposes during
the climax. The coda is serene in comparison to the immediately preceding
music, but it has an ambiguous, questioning quality of its own that leaves

us with Ives's trademark, another open ending. This open ending is especially necessary to Ives's stylistic and formal conception, since the traditional style cannot by itself be permitted to fully resolve the song's range of experiences any more than the other style could in isolation be allowed to conclude the piece.

Thus, Ives does not allow the reminiscence of his traditional style in the coda to sound truly conclusive or to proceed very far. The C♯–G♯ pedal point, which plays such an important role in the original foreground style, returns in the coda—but a deliberate ambiguity between C♯ minor and C♯ major (the latter implied by the F♯ in the left hand of the piano part) freshens the sound and precludes any ultimate feeling of resolution. The "Contented river" motive is restated here in the right hand of the piano part. However, the motive's concluding E comes to rest not on anything like a tonic chord but rather on a sensuous ninth chord built on F♯, in which the melodic E provides the seventh. This is a "good place to stop, not end," and at this point Ives allows his piece to drift into a tantalizing silence.

Somewhere within that silence, within the mind of the sensitive listener, the two styles of "The Housatonic at Stockbridge" may continue to coexist and develop, and perhaps even interact in new and unforeseen ways. Like the multifaceted river itself, the larger natural world of which the river forms a part, and the universe of thought inspired by these phenomena, this music by implication never truly ends.

To culminate a layered piece by separating and juxtaposing its styles, as Ives does in "The Housatonic at Stockbridge," is an inspired approach to giving the piece an overall formal shape. This culmination is not typical of Ives's other layered pieces, but I'm not sure anything is "typical" of them. In *The Unanswered Question*, one of the three superimposed stylistic layers reaches a climax and ends its role in the piece, while the remaining two continue—unruffled, unreconciled and, by implication, unendingly, on through eternity. In *Central Park in the Dark,* one of the two layers reaches a frenzied climax and stops, only to re-emerge quietly against the other layer just before the end of the piece, in what could be either a reminiscence, or a resurgence of the entire cycle. In the scherzo of the Fourth Symphony, the multilayered strands eventually explode into a kind of communal celebration marked by patriotic-sounding chaos, until the music literally collapses from its own weight. All of these pieces invite and even demand reflection of the most intense and provocative nature; multilayered meanings emerge from experiencing these inspired instances of stylistic layering.

Ives's brief, epigrammatic song, "The Cage," offers an instructive example of his use of layered elements to construct a *single* composite style. Comparison with "The Housatonic at Stockbridge" will clearly show the differences between this technique and the layering of discrete styles.

NOTE:- All notes not marked with sharp or flat are natural.

EXAMPLE 7–5. Ives, "The Cage," complete.

Copyright © 1955 by Peer International Corporation.
Used by Permission.

"The Cage" is shown in its entirety in Ex. 7–5. The piano part of the song is based principally upon chords built from stacked perfect fourths. The vocal line consists almost entirely of whole-tone scale segments, and alternates pitch groups chosen from one of the two whole-tone scales with pitch groups chosen from the other. Since a whole-tone scale contains no perfect fourths, it is apparent that the voice and piano parts are constructed along different lines. Yet together they create a unified, rather than dichotomous, impression. A careful look at the score will reveal a number of reasons why this is so.

Although the song has no traditional sense of meter, the voice and the accompaniment maintain a feeling of rhythmic alignment throughout the song. "The Cage" never approaches the feeling of two completely independent rhythmic layers, which characterizes the music of "The Housatonic at Stockbridge." Perhaps more significantly, the many points of exact rhythmic alignment in "The Cage"—when the voice and the piano attack notes together—are almost always points of pitch alignment as well, where the vocal pitch will also be found within the piano's chord. (In the two cases that constitute the only exceptions to this, on the words "back" and "when," the following vocal pitch is a member of the piano's chord.) This pitch alignment helps the singer, of course, but in so doing assures a real and continuing sense of ensemble between the performers that cannot help but communicate itself to the listener as well. Unlike "The Housatonic at Stockbridge," the music of "The Cage" is constructed so as to emphasize continuously the points of congruence between its two different pitch systems.

"The Cage" continues its single composite style throughout its brief duration, and it is thus a splendid illustration of how unified and consistent an effect Ives could achieve on those occasions when he wanted to do so. Ives here espouses a traditional aesthetic of stylistic unity. The obsessive, unrelieved, intentionally monotonous effect Ives desires here makes such a "traditional" approach necessary. This approach does not, however, preclude the composer's employment of yet another open ending, which is paired with an actual question in Ives's text. The vocal line seems to begin all over again on the words "Is life anything like that?" with the accompaniment providing the same chords and rhythmic pattern as it did for the opening vocal phrase; but both voice and piano stop abruptly as soon as the question is out. The verbal and musical unanswered question hangs in the shocked silence, lingering beyond the point where the piece stops—as Ives's fermata clearly indicates.

There are many subtleties to admire in this darkly sardonic little song. The vocal line in "The Cage" circles back and forth aimlessly, like the leopard it is describing; it seemingly "bumps" at intervals against the leaden piano chords, which may well be taken to suggest something like the bars of a cage. (These chords even look something like cage bars in Ives's score.) Ives's way of working with his stylistic material is obviously appropriate for the subject of this song, since the piece offers two distinctive kinds of musical vocabulary inextricably bound together in a powerful, if artificially imposed, unity.

Song

Both "The Housatonic at Stockbridge" and "The Cage" started their musical lives as instrumental pieces, and were arranged as songs afterwards. This seems a strange reversal of the expected process, especially in the case of "The Housatonic at Stockbridge." Robert Underwood Johnson's poem is included as an epigraph to the orchestral score of "The Housatonic"; still, it is entirely possible to hear the orchestral work with deep appreciation without realizing that its main melody line is a setting of that poem.

"The Housatonic at Stockbridge" and "The Cage" are not isolated instances; the interrelationships between Ives's instrumental works and his vocal works run numerous and deep. There are no indications at all in the score of the huge *Browning* Overture that a portion of the work might be a song in disguise, yet listeners familiar with the overture will recognize part of it in the later song "From 'Paracelsus,'" which in fact is a setting of a Browning text. Ives offers optional parts for viola and flute in the score of his "Concord" Sonata, but leaves no clue in this score that a portion of its "Thoreau" movement forms the basis for a highly evocative song. When we turn to Ives's Violin Sonatas, which contain instrumental treatments of pre-existing hymns, the composer's arrangement of some relevant excerpts from them as songs is not surprising. However, it is surprising, and noteworthy, that the song Ives derived from the final movement of his hymn-inspired Symphony No. 3 contains much more of that movement's music than just the portion literally based on "Just As I Am Without One Plea."

Ives may have felt at first that his more demanding musical conceptions would meet more resistance from singers than from instrumentalists, and so he chose purely instrumental settings for some works that originated as vocal inspirations. In the case of "The Housatonic," Ives doubtless selected the orchestral medium because his musical vision was conveyed with the least compromise in that setting (as the note on the first page of the song version indicates). He doubtless chose to make it a "song without voice" because no singer could hold the main line against the big orchestral climax just before the end. Later on, when he was compiling his songbook, and performances of his instrumental music did not seem to be forthcoming, he may have felt that some of his music could be returned to its vocal source of inspiration and presented in the traditionally accessible format of songs for voice and piano.

The sheer quantity of Ives's explicitly vocal output is staggering; there are far more individual works for voice than there are individual works of any other type, and Ives produced vocal music throughout his career. Our earliest existing Ives pieces are vocal and the last works he completed were songs. In addition, a number of Ives's largest and most important instrumental works incorporate optional or nonoptional choral parts: the final "Thanksgiving" movement of the *Holidays* Symphony; the final movement of the Second Orchestral Set (entitled "From Hanover Square North, at the End of a Tragic Day, the Voice of the People Again Arose"); and the first and last movements of the Fourth Symphony.

However, the importance of song for Ives transcends issues relating to his choice of performance medium. Consider how frequently Ives quoted, or alluded to, song or obvious song styles in his instrumental as well as his vocal work; Ives's musical quotations are comprised overwhelmingly of songs. The conclusion seems inescapable that, in a sense, Ives was almost always writing songs, or at least writing *about* song. Why was song so important to Charles Ives?

One answer is that Ives, as a thinker, as a writer, and above all as a musician, was immersed in the shaping, articulation, and nuances of his native language. This is reflected both in his vocal and in his nonvocal music. Ives's songs reveal a remarkable sensitivity to the rhythms and inflections of the English language, particularly those of American English in many shades of both formal and casual expression. On the other hand, the fluid, asymmetrical phrasing and the occasionally jerky rhythms of the melodic lines in Ives's instrumental works are traits they share with the vocal lines of many of his most representative songs. It is not difficult to imagine the opening section of a piece like "Decoration Day" as a "setting" of a typically Ivesian, but in this case unstated, text. By this I do not mean that the music implies a *specific* text; rather, that it celebrates the essential and characteristic gestures of American speech and expression, and therefore also of Ivesian song. If we can accept this music, and many other instrumental passages in Ives's oeuvre, as representative in this way, much of the apparent peculiarity and willfulness of the melodic line and the rhythmic articulation dissolves.

Much has been written of the relationships certain innovative musical languages in our century establish with crucial characteristics of their creators' native languages and cultures. To mention just two examples: Debussy's radical approach to phrase structure and rhythm has been linked many times to traits of French language and literature; and the idiosyncratic rhythms and melodic inflections of Bartók's music are an obvious product and byproduct of that composer's assimilation of Hungarian and other peasant culture. I think Ives could well be added to this list.

But song, and evocations and celebrations of the act of singing, were important to Ives for reasons even beyond the ones already discussed. We know of Ives's artistic isolation in the social and cultural climate of his time and place. We know also how often he wrote of the excitement and inspiration he derived early in life from the experience and the sounds of small-town, nonprofessional, *communal* music-making. Much of this communal music-making involved group song. Others might emphasize a nostalgic aspect in Ives's immersion in song, but I prefer to view that immersion in a more outward-directed and open-ended way. I think that by evoking and celebrating song in his music, both literally and by stylistic implication, Ives was creating *in his work* the community that was missing for him in the milieu that he found outside it.

With song, Ives conjured imaginatively, and reached out toward the musical community he so longed for—not the community of his childhood, but the community that would understand and participate in the creative work of his adulthood. Here is perhaps the ultimate significance of Ives's fascination with, and obvious need for, song. (Can it merely coincidence that the song which Ives selected to open his huge and extraordinary songbook, "Majority"—a work which in many ways is his "biggest" song—represents a paean to the community of all humankind?)

Ives's use and evocation of song is an act of creative courage and aspiration that invites the *listener* to participate in the creation of a community in which Ives's music can live and thrive. By appreciating and partaking in his celebration of song, we respond personally and meaningfully to the impulse toward community that animates so much of his music; symbolically we join with other listeners, and even with Ives, as at least potential members of his idealized community. Of course we cannot literally reach across time to relieve the composer's intense isolation, which caused him so much anguish. But we can reach toward his music, which so obviously longs for *us,* and in so doing vindicate the work of this extraordinary artist and the significance of that work, demonstrating that Ives's efforts to create a community in, and for, his music were not in vain.

8

The Structuring of Styles: Additional Alternatives

As this investigation of style in the music of Ives approaches a "good place to stop, not end," some further observations should be made about the overall form of Ives's stylistically heterogeneous works. Most of the pieces discussed in the preceding chapters return in their ending passages to their stylistic points of departure, or at least make some reference, however veiled, to the traditional formal principle of a rounded ending. Of course, Ives's rounded endings nearly always contain the seeds of their own subversion, due to the presence of elements in them that also preclude any traditional sense of absolute closure: alterations in the original pitch level or pitch structures, the addition of new and ambiguous elements, and so forth. Nevertheless, the expectation of some kind of structural return is so basic to most people's experience of music that it is not surprising to find Ives utilizing, and playing with, that expectation much of the time.

Not all of Ives's pieces behave this way, however. In this chapter, I wish briefly to explore two approaches to structuring stylistic progression that have not yet been discussed as ways of shaping entire works. One of these is stylistic "simplification." The other is its opposite, which I shall call stylistic "complexifying."

Stylistic simplification and complexifying have already been encountered as aspects of pieces that ultimately employ, or allude to, the principle of stylistic return. The first piece analyzed in this book, "Ann Street," was described in terms of a stylistic arch, which employed first accelerating complexity of style and then a gradual return to simpler idioms. Few Ives pieces demonstrate as smooth and relatively symmetrical a stylistic arch as "Ann Street," but all of Ives's stylistically varied works inevitably demonstrate either some simplification or some complexifying of style, if not both. A work like "Decoration Day" clearly employs the gradual simplification of style as a structuring element; it is only at the last minute, literally, that the piece breaks this pattern in favor of an abrupt return back to the opening complex style.

Ives's song "Majority" may be cited as an example of a work whose overall form is determined by stylistic simplification. It is a massive piece about "the masses" of humanity, with music encompassing a variety of stylistic effects ranging from huge tone clusters to pure triads. Ives selected this work to open his book of *114 Songs*, in order to "give all the 'old girls' another ride," as he inimitably put it, but surely also for more substantial reasons. The song seems to present an overview of Ives's entire world of musical styles, set to a text by the composer that communicates significant aspects of his own world view:

> The Masses! The Masses!
> The Masses have toiled,
> Behold the works of the World!
> The Masses are thinking,
> Whence comes the thought of the World!
> The Masses are singing,
> Whence comes the Art of the World!
> The Masses are yearning,
> Whence comes the hope of the World.
> The Masses are dreaming,
> Whence comes the visions of God!
> God's in His Heaven,
> All will be well with the World!

It must have been very important to Ives that he find an original and convincing formal shape for this ambitious populist credo. The plan that evolved demonstrates a gradual simplification of style from the beginning of the piece right up to the final chords.

"Majority" opens with a long piano introduction, thrusting the listener immediately into an unmetered, thickly textured, disjunct, dissonant, and nontonal music of exceptional complexity (Ex. 8–1.) The enormous tone clusters serve as a virtually literal portrayal of "masses," and they form

* Preferably for a unison chorus; it is almost impossible for a single voice to hold the part against the score.

EXAMPLE 8–1. Ives, "Majority," mm. 1–9.

From: Nineteen Songs.
Copyright © 1935 Merion Music, Inc.
Used By Permission Of The Publisher.

the basis of the accompaniment when the voice enters at last, proclaiming that very word. As the text continues to reveal the importance and the capabilities of the human masses, the tone clusters disappear, yielding place to a series of well-differentiated musical idioms. Each of these styles is focused upon specific, limited intervals and rhythms, and is characterized by a particular texture and use of register. Each of the styles can also be related in some fashion to elements presented during the introduction, as might be expected in an Ives piece. (The musical corollary these procedures create with the evolution of ideas in the text is apparent.)

Example 8–2 shows two of these styles, and gives some indication of how more complex styles yield place to less complex ones as the song progresses. "The Masses have toiled" is set to thick, highly dissonant, heavily accented chords, which struggle gradually upward (and downward) in ponderous, square rhythms. "The Masses are singing" is set to gentler, repetitive patterns in a lilting 6/8 meter, with softer dynamics, a less dense texture, and even a hint of folk-like melisma in the diatonic vocal part. Ives is too sophisticated a composer to make the process of stylistic simplification an absolutely linear one, but over the course of the song there is no mistaking the movement toward greater simplicity.

The last page of the piece is shown in Ex. 8–3. The final gesture of the song is a triadic cadence figure on "the World," but it will be noticed that the music does not arrive at this ending without first summarizing the stylistic journey that has brought it to this point. A black-key tone cluster akin to those heard right at the beginning of the piece is played several times in the measures just before the song's conclusion, and the white-key chords played by the left hand in these same measures are also obviously cluster-like. In the last three measures, a chromatic progression of triads, and a dense chord reminiscent in sound and structure of many heard earlier in the piece, directly precede the two cadential chords.

The last two chords of "Majority" present the only traditional triadic *progression* in the piece. But is this really a conventional final cadence? I

EXAMPLE 8–2. Ives, "Majority," mm. 10–12; 17–22.

From: Nineteen Songs.
Copyright © 1935 Merion Music, Inc.
Used By Permission Of The Publisher.

EXAMPLE 8–3. Ives, "Majority," mm. 36–45.

From: Nineteen Songs.
Copyright © 1935 Merion Music, Inc.
Used By Permission Of The Publisher.

think not. To hear it as a V–I progression in F major would seem to be a mistake and a subversion of Ives's intent. The vocal line, after all, makes its cadence to the note C. The position of the melody, and of all the other chordal voices as well, strongly suggests a I–IV progression in C major— an incomplete "Amen" cadence! Note the final descrescendo. The "missing" C–major chord, which would truly end the piece, can occur only in the imagination, out of earshot, in some distant realm of the mind. So, along with the simplification, Ives produces another open ending. After all, "All *will* be well with the World," but all is not well with the world *yet*. Ives's ending is one that points directly toward resolution, but also leaves us with an awareness of the need for further action.

Significantly, triads do not occur only at the ending of "Majority." Just as the song's beginning is recalled shortly before it concludes, so the ending sonorities are forecast earlier in the piece. This helps assure that the final triads will not seem excessively simplistic and arbitrary—a danger Ives approaches perilously in "Majority," but which I think he manages to avoid.

It is shown in Ex. 8–3 that distinct, isolated triads occur at the first articulation of the word "God"—although the adjacency of the left- and right-hand triads at this point helps Ives avoid any premature sense of traditional tonal progression and creates a chromatic blurring of the chords, giving this measure some continuity with the immediately preceding music. However, this is not the first time triads are clearly heard in this piece; again, Ives is too skillful a composer to wait until we are nearly at the end of the song to lay the groundwork for its eventual stylistic goal. Parallel triads are heard considerably earlier, prominently and unambiguously, with the phrase "Whence comes the Art of the World!" At this earlier point, the stylistic simplification does seem too abrupt, but I think this effect is deliberate on Ives's part. The triads certainly call a fanfare-like attention to "the Art of the World," but the gesture seems self-conscious and pompous. The listener is being manipulated here to feel that some reversion to greater complexity and a more extensive spinning-out of the simplification process will be required before a truly satisfying ending can be achieved. He is also being prepared to accept a triadic ending as a logical and preordained development when it does come.

Other examples may be found among Ives's songs of overall forms based upon stylistic simplification. Both "Down East" and "Old Home Day," referred to by Ives as "Street Songs," demonstrate this structuring procedure. "Down East" divides obviously into two parts; the first part serves as a kind of dissonant, intensely chromatic introduction and foil to the consonant, diatonic second. (The division of styles in "Down East" is not absolute, however, and references back to the chromaticism and complex dissonance of the opening section seep into the second part at critical points to generate a fine feeling of poignancy, as well as structural subtlety and stylistic integration.) "Old Home Day" falls clearly into three sections: the first dissonant, chromatic, and nontonal; the second relatively more consonant and pitch-centered, with a mixture of diatonic and chromatic elements; and the last a lively march in G major. The similarity in stylistic structure between "Old Home Day" and the three main sections of "Decoration Day" is apparent; the march in the song is even introduced via a transition with drum-like chords that directly recalls the transition into the march in the orchestral work.

Works by Ives that demonstrate structural complexifying in a pure, unadulterated way are not common. This is probably due to the frequently-remarked tendency of Ives's music to begin at more complicated, rather than simpler, stages of development. However, two of Ives's shortest (but also most beautiful) songs do exemplify the complexifying process.

"Maple Leaves" begins in a stylistic condition close to that of pure diatonicism, but undergoes a sea change as the leaves described in the song first turn to gold and then fall from the tree. The piece is shown as Ex. 8–4. At the word "gold," sung on a wonderfully unexpected D♯, the apparently passing and anomalous touches of chromaticism in the first two measures of the piano part suddenly intensify and virtually take over the language of the piece. The rest of the music consists of ultimately unsuccessful efforts to constrain this chromaticism and to restore some feeling of consonance or pitch center.

First, on the line beginning "The most are gone now," the piano attempts to stabilize its music into repeated ostinato figures. Then, as movement inevitably begins again on "Soon these will slip from out the twig's weak hold," the accompaniment recalls the arpeggiated phrases with which it began, as the voice also recalls its opening phrase. But here, despite the occasional broken triads which occur in the piano, the general level of dissonance and chromaticism has become too great to restore any feeling of a diatonic norm or tonal center. It is as if the music has reversed the stylistic condition that prevailed at the opening of the piece, and the passing diatonic elements now seem intrusions within the essentially chromatic context. As the piece approaches its end, notice how the voice becomes chromatically serpentine, and at last, unable to "linger" any longer, it surrenders completely to the downward pull of an unadorned chromatic scale, while the piano figuration dissolves upward in chromatic steps of its own, which are spaced as major sevenths. The stylistic progression, and the matching of this with the progression of the Aldrich poem, could not be more artfully or movingly executed. Considering the wide stylistic range traversed by the song within its very brief duration, the feeling of gentle inevitability that it achieves is particularly admirable.

Song number 12 in *114 Songs*, which is called "Remembrance" in the

Thomas Bailey Aldrich*

EXAMPLE 8–4. Ives, "Maple Leaves," complete.

book's index but which bears no title on the score page, is Ives's compact and extraordinary tribute to the memory of his father. It is shown in Ex. 8–5. Until its last two measures, the piece is almost Spartan in its simplicity of vocabulary and texture, and one might never suspect that this song is derived from a chamber work, "The Pond," which has a lush and densely layered texture. The two works are ultimately quite different both in stylistic structure and in aesthetic impact, but despite the sumptuous and evocative musical imagery of "The Pond," the song arguably makes a more penetratingly direct statement.

Up to the final two measures, the song uses only the notes of a G-major scale. The voice and the upper register of the keyboard intone a purely diatonic and basically stepwise melody, in canon one measure and one octave apart. This is accompanied by flowing arpeggiated figures that imply tonic and subdominant harmonies in G, "shadowed" slightly by the extended stacking of open fifths on the G and by the presence of the major seventh above the C, but not really obscured. (The perfect fifths suggest an "open" acoustic, perhaps akin to that produced by open horn tones sounding across a small body of water.) The pianissimo dynamic level specified by Ives helps assure that the effect of the stacked fifths will be one of gentleness, and the indicated pedaling helps assure a blending of sounds in which there will be no real feeling of dissonance.

This delicate, but strictly controlled, framework suddenly breaks open in the final two measures, as Ives produces a breathtaking emotional impact from a handful of unexpected, colorful chords. For the first time in the piece, more than two notes are heard simultaneously in the piano part, and the impression created of a sudden fullness and intensity is remarkable; furthermore, the abrupt embracing of even mild chromaticism in the music suggests, in context, an expressive and stylistic liberation of almost unbounded extent. All this reflects musically, of course, the meaning and importance to Ives of his "father's song." The voice hangs on these central words, and on the unresolved note A, in an open ending which bespeaks the importance, the elusiveness, and the persistence of memory.

Ives's final touch, an ascending perfect fourth from C♯ to F♯ in the high register of the piano, accomplishes several structural and expressive tasks in one small gesture. The perfect fourth refers back to earlier aspects of the accompaniment: the perfect fifths (C♯ to F♯ is an inverted perfect fifth); the repeated upper F♯ in the arpeggios of the first three measures; and the register used for the piano's imitation of the vocal melody (where one may trace a gradual stepwise ascent from D to E to the final F♯ in the highest notes of the melodic phrases). However, while recalling where we have been stylistically, and thus providing a small reference to formal rounding and integration, this ending gesture also reveals the stylistic and expressive distance we have suddenly traveled from the earlier music, as both the C♯

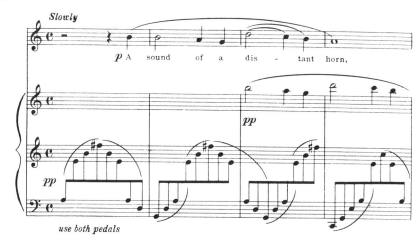

"The music in my heart I bore
Long after it was heard no more."
Wordsworth.

EXAMPLE 8–5. Ives, "Remembrance," complete.

Copyright © 1954 by Peer International Corporation.
Used by Permission.

142

and the F$^\sharp$ clash pointedly with the chord underlying them. The F$^\sharp$ against the F$^\natural$ yields a particularly telling dissonance on which to end; obviously, memory brings the pain of loss along with deepened understanding. (And, if all this is not enough, the listener may also recognize in the pattern of two C$^\sharp$s moving to a lone F$^\sharp$ a reference to "Taps," as if this motive of farewell is what is heard from the "distant horn.")

This little song reveals an inspiring ability on Ives's part to distill musical gesture and meaning down to the purest essence. Every note in this piece is distinctly heard and clearly functional. The piece has a jewel-like integrity that opens, for once, the intriguing possibility of Ives as a "perfectionist"—nothing messy here! On the other hand, despite the extreme refinement of means, the attitude toward style that is manifested in the song reveals it to be in every way a work representative of Charles Ives. It may not be a "typical" Ives piece, whatever that is, but would be impossible to conceive of any other likely composer for it, not only because of what it accomplishes stylistically and expressively, but because it achieves those ends so daringly, and so well.

Perfectionism and "Serenity"

There are, in fact, pieces by Ives—always short pieces of very special expressive intent—that lend credence to the apparently bizarre notion of Ives as a perfectionist. Almost all of them are songs, several of which exist also in instrumental versions as parts of the various "sets" for chamber ensemble assembled or planned by Ives at different stages in his compositional career. Such pieces show that, when he wanted to, Ives could write music as carefully controlled and homogeneous as any "great" composer could; the point seems to be that he didn't want to do this very much of the time.

As an example of Ives's "perfectionism," I would choose "Serenity," a product of the composer's full maturity that is so uncharacteristically extreme in its restriction of musical materials and style that it could well give a contemporary minimalist composer pause for thought (and envy). The complete song is shown in Ex. 8–6. Ives's *Memos* indicate that at one point he was going to include this song on a list of his weaker pieces, but apparently he decided against it and crossed "Serenity" off the list. I'm glad he did; the song is surely atypical, but it is not unworthy of Ives. In fact, even in "Serenity," as in other stylistically restrained pieces by Ives, the creator's "fingerprints" are unquestionably present.

The vocal line of "Serenity" is essentially a chant. With the exception of a single B$^\flat$, it avoids any chromaticism; and with the exception of two small

John Greenleaf Whittier
(from *The Brewing of Soma*)

EXAMPLE 8–6. Ives, "Serenity," complete.

leaps of a third just preceding and just following the significant word "ordered"—which also marks the single high point of the line on the note E—it adheres to purely stepwise motion. The range of the voice remains within a single octave throughout the song, and its line establishes a feeling of clear pitch centers, first on A and then, in the final measures of the song, on B.

The accompaniment is, if anything, even more restricted in its material than the voice. The piano is given a basic repertoire of two chords, which remain fixed in register throughout, and maintain exactly the same rhythmic pattern and relationship until very close to the end of the song. Even these two chords share a close kinship. They have a common pitch, B, and except for one note in each they are actually transpositions of each other (as the C♯-G-B of the second chord represents the pitches B-F-A of the first chord moved up a whole step.) The pitches used in the two chords, with the exception of the C♯, are all pitches that appear in the vocal line, so there is a sense of harmonic congruence between voice and accompaniment for the duration of the song. This congruence extends to a significant structural detail. The motion "up" a whole step, suggested by the opening relationship of the piano's two chords, forecasts, in effect, the overall movement of the voice upward by a whole step, from a center on A to a center on B. Furthermore, as if to underscore the importance of this, the two piano chords exchange their metrical position at the point in the song where the voice definitively shifts its center upward: in m. 19, the C♯ chord at last attains downbeat status.

The sense of clear purpose with which Ives establishes and maintains the style he invented for this song is admirable, while the expressive resources he uncovers in this apparently limited style are remarkable. Many of these expressive resources have to do with the relationships Ives is able to forge between his music and the words of Whittier's poem. The free alternation between duple and triple subdivisions of the beat in the voice part reflects Ives's attention to the most minute details of text rhythm and accentuation, while the absolute regularity of the dotted quarter-note pulse in the accompaniment permits these details of text-rhythm to be perceived by the listener and to achieve maximum expressive impact. Even within the highly restricted accompaniment itself, the main point of alteration, where the two basic chords exchange metrical positions, is placed significantly with respect to the text of the song. The exchange takes place as the "strain and stress" are taken from our souls; the momentary acceleration of rhythmic activity in the accompaniment in m. 18 presumably reflects the act of removing the tension. It is very effective that, as a result of this exchange, from m. 19 onward the less dissonant of the two basic chords falls on the downbeat, rather than vice versa. In this restrictive context, the change is clearly heard, and one may actually experience the lessening of "strain and stress." (The B-F-A-C chord contains, and is framed by, a dissonant minor ninth, while the C♯-G-B-E chord is framed by a consonant minor third, and has no minor ninth.) Measures 18–19 also mark the point in the song where the vocal line moves up to its new center on B; in context, the line seems to invite us to rise with it to a new plane of spirituality and awareness, where our lives will be newly "ordered" and peaceful.

Ives's severe limiting of material, and his tight control over what material there is, extends in "Serenity" even into the realms of dynamics and tempo, as the composer's rather extensive opening directions clearly indicate. But this is not quite early "trance music." Deviations from the restricted style of the opening measures do occur in "Serenity." They are so subtle, so smooth, and so well integrated into the fabric of the piece that they hardly qualify as interruptions or juxtapositions, but they are there nevertheless. They identify the composer of the piece, certainly. But what is much more important is that they contribute immeasurably to the song's beauty, depth, and effectiveness—which is why they are there. We cannot forget that Ives's employment of stylistic features is always, inevitably, linked to his concerns with substance.

Stylistic deviations take place in mm. 11 and 22. These measures occupy analogous positions in the song's structure; each immediately precedes the concluding word of a poetic stanza, which is marked in turn by a cadential long note in the vocal line. The two measures of music are themselves analogous as well, with m. 22 being a transposition up a whole step of m. 11.

From a purely musical standpoint, these two gently anomalous measures present Ives's ingenious solution to the problem of how one creates effective cadences in a piece with such a limited style. And in terms of the text, Ives obviously wants to set off the crucial words "love" and "peace." By deviating from the established style just *before* each of these two words, he creates the sense of an important structural event when the style returns to accompany the words. The stylistic deviations function like arrows, pointing up the cadences and their crucial words to our special attention. In context, the music for "love" and "peace" becomes paradoxically reinvigorated.

Some of this effect of reinvigoration has to do with the specific style Ives chooses for mm. 11 and 22. They feature triadic structures that suggest traditional four-part hymn-book harmony: little "Amen" cadence formulas, with just a touch of passing chromaticism. I will offer in a moment some explanation for why these measures don't sound more disruptive than they do. But clearly, surrounded as they are with the much more severe style that dominates "Serenity," these measures have a rather clichéd effect. One is made to appreciate how much stronger and more expressive by comparison are the chords Ives uses for his actual cadences on "love" and "peace," breathing (with the vocalist) a sigh of relief that Ives did not place further conventional triads on these words. By extension, one comes at these points to appreciate with renewed intensity the appropriateness of the basic style Ives uses to express the religious sentiments of the song as a whole.

Once again, then, Ives is suggesting in "Serenity" the extent to which our perceptions and experiences of style, and the meanings we assign to style, are contextual and comparative in nature. He is also showing us the extent to which these contextual and comparative aspects of style form the basis of how he constructs his music.

A look at m. 11 will help clarify why the momentary stylistic alteration here seems so smooth and seamless. Only two new pitches are introduced into the piece in this measure: $B^\flat$ and D. Essential rhythmic and registral aspects of the music do not change here, except for the fact that the voice is doubled by the accompaniment. As for the F-major triad that dominates the harmony of this measure, not only are its individual pitches not new to the piece, but we have in fact been hearing the notes of an F-major triad continually, on every downbeat since the opening of the piece, as part of the B-F-A-C chord. The material of m. 22 is equally nondisruptive, for analogous reasons.

A word is in order on the final chord of "Serenity." It is a "perfect" concluding sonority from a number of standpoints. Combining aspects of the song's two essential chords, it preserves the intervallic structure of the C#-G-B-E chord, but transposes this structure back *down* a whole step, so that its lowest note is B; B has, of course, been important throughout the song as the lowest note of the other essential chord, and as the common tone shared by the two basic chords. The importance of B in the final rolled chord of "Serenity" is doubly appropriate, of course, since B emerges as the central pitch and the cadential tone of the vocal line in the concluding measures. Any residual tension that might have persisted into the final measures from the "conflict" between C# and C♮ in the progression of the two basic chords is, in effect, resolved by the absence of both of these pitches in the concluding sonority. This last chord is voiced so that its highest pitch, D, may be heard as a central and restful arrival point for the constant oscillation between high C and E, which results from the alternation and voicing of the two basic chords.

"Serenity" is a very special piece in the Ives oeuvre, as its title indicates; it is meant to describe a rare condition that Ives evokes only rarely. For all of Ives's deep religious fervor, it is ultimately the problematic activities of earthly existence that tend to color his work, much more than portrayals of pure religious apotheosis or other possibly "perfect" states of being. (It has been seen, with both "General William Booth Enters Into Heaven" and "Majority," how even works that deal in some ways with religious apotheosis may remain ultimately and surprisingly tied to the imperfect earth.) This suggests why Ives was so rarely interested in being a "perfectionist." Still, it was a possibility he occasionally investigated, and those who are most comfortable with conventional ideals of artistic control and unity may take some comfort from the existence of pieces like "Serenity" in the Ives oeuvre, and may be able to see in them proof of Ives's "seriousness" as an artist—perhaps also using them as points of departure for the investigation of more characteristic, "messier" Ives works. In any case, the composer who could place both "Serenity" and "Majority" in the same songbook could well proclaim, along with Whitman:

> Do I contradict myself?
> Very well then I contradict myself,
> (I am large, I contain multitudes.)

Postlude: Is Ives a Great Composer?

All too often, deliberations about "greatness," with their frequently attendant rankings of artists and listings of "masterpieces," are demonstrations of critical chutzpah rather than critical insight. Obviously, Ives is an *important* composer. Personally, I find him too important to spend much time worrying about whether he is a "great" composer. His work keeps me too busy with substantive issues. I think Ives would have been happy with this evaluation, would have hoped that others might share it, and would have encouraged us to drop the matter right there.

However, it is worthwhile to ponder why the issue of Ives's "greatness" seems to arise so readily, even so innocently. It may be because the qualities, which for many constitute "greatness," have, all too often, more to do with aspects of artistic manner than with what Ives would be willing to call aspects of artistic substance. In any case, Ives does not fit gracefully into a list of obviously "great" composers, whether that list is headed by Bach, Mozart, and Beethoven, or Debussy, Stravinsky, and Schoenberg.

One factor here is the problematic state in which Ives maintained and left much of his oeuvre. Shouldn't a "great" artist have exercised more care over his works of art, bringing at least most of them to an obviously finished and final state? But the condition of the oeuvre brings up a deeper issue, which may offer the best rationale yet for Ives's apparent "outsider" status vis-à-vis the pantheon of our unequivocally "great" composers. For one must suspect that the "work of art" itself was not the matter of highest importance to Ives, and that, for Ives, art was ultimately a *means* to a spiritual and intangible end, not the end itself.

It is hard to be entirely comfortable with this. Ives's ideals, while obviously admirable, conflict with much of what our culture teaches about art and the way our culture is inclined to regard and use art. We tend to glorify individual works; to worship their eloquence, grace, and fineness of form—their "perfection," in other words; and to lionize as "great" those individuals who provide us with appropriate aesthetic icons according to these criteria. But the production of icons is not what Ives ever had in mind.

Perhaps then Ives truly belongs with the "concept" artists, those for whom the *idea*, rather than the artistic means that convey it, is the only important thing. Yet Ives appears no more at home on a list of dadaists or futurists than he does on other lists; he doesn't seem to belong with Satie or Cage, say, any more than he belongs with Wagner or Elliott Carter. The comparison with John Cage is especially instructive. In much of Cage's "aleatoric" music from the 1950s and later, the idea is really the piece. An individual realization of the work is a passing event, not to be repeated, and useful only insofar as it is representative of certain underlying concerns that constitute the real "piece." But Ives's works are not *merely* passing means to an end in this same sense. The individual sound experiences in Ives are not negligible, freely interchangeable, or disposable; they have been endowed deliberately with individual, specifically expressive, and traditionally "artistic" qualities. However (and here he is a bit more like Cage, perhaps, than like a more traditional artist), Ives offers these sound experiences not to inspire our admiration of them, or of himself as creator. They are offered as spurs to the "activity of truth."

Ives's works represent aspects of a *process*, both for him and for his intended audience, but they are essential aspects of that process. They are a means of engaging issues of the utmost seriousness and importance. And they are wondrous, frequently beautiful, means of engaging these issues, which is why they are so successful at it. Viewed in this way, Ives seems to eat his cake and have it too. Without having posited the making of "works of art" as an ultimate goal, he managed to make a number of them anyway, and a number of very fine ("great?") ones. (No wonder many professional musicians remain suspicious and distrustful of this man!)

So, maybe Ives is a "great" composer, and maybe he isn't. Let's suppose, for the sake of putting the matter to rest, that in the final analysis he isn't. Then I would have to conclude by asserting that, given the significance of the issues raised by his work and the success with which his work raises them, perhaps Ives was after something more important than being a "great" composer. It just may be that the oeuvre of Ives, even if it doesn't achieve "greatness," achieves something that is more important than our traditional ideal of intrinsic "greatness."

There is always something more to be said.

—*Charles Ives, as quoted by the Cowells*

Notes

[The numbers in brackets following a short title refer to the page number of its original, complete citation in these Notes.]

PRELUDE

PAGE

2   "Manner" and "substance": for Ives's ideas about "manner" and "substance" in art, see p. 17.

STYLE AND SUBSTANCE

6   I had the good fortune to study with George Perle at Queens College, CUNY, and his remark on Ives remains with me after some 25 years. For the Ives quotation, see Vivian Perlis's *Charles Ives Remembered: An Oral History* (New Haven and London: Yale University Press, 1974), p. 40.

11   Mahler: On the kinships between Ives and Mahler, see Robert P. Morgan's "Ives and Mahler: Mutual Responses at the End of an Era," in *19th-Century Music* Vol. 2 (1978), pp. 72–81.

11   Stravinsky: There are two significant exceptions to my generalization about the homogeneity of style in individual Stravinsky works. One is *Petrouchka*, where stylistic dichotomies are part of an elaborate programmatic scenario; the other is *Agon*, in every way an anomalous, albeit fascinating, piece in Stravinsky's output, which was completed years after Ives had stopped composing. Elsewhere in Stravinsky's oeuvre, we may find various substyles explored within a given piece, but there is nothing suggesting the kinds of stylistic procedures employed frequently by Ives.

14   Ives's *Essays Before A Sonata* may be found in the anthology *Essays Before A*

Sonata, The Majority, and Other Writings by Charles Ives, ed. Howard Boatwright (New York: Norton, 1970). The "Orderly reason . . ." passage is in the "Emerson" portion of the *Essays,* on p. 22 of this edition.

14   The Carter quotation is from Perlis [6], p. 145.

15   Crumb and Rochberg: For Crumb's use of quotation, see works such as *Makrokosmos,* Vol. I, for piano, which quotes Chopin, or *Ancient Voices of Children,* for two voices and chamber ensemble, which quotes Bach. Rochberg's "carefully patterned alternations of style" are well illustrated in his String Quartet No. 3.

15   Carter: This is a continuation of the passage from the interview in Perlis [6], p. 145.

INTO ANALYSIS

17   The Ives quotations are from Section III of the epilogue, in Boatwright's *Essays Before A Sonata, The Majority, and Other Writings by Charles Ives* [14], pp. 75 and 77.

JUXTAPOSITION AND SEQUENCE (I): A WALK ON "ANN STREET"

20   "Ann Street" is song 25 in Ives's *114 Songs;* the collection is now available in a reprint of Ives's original 1922 edition (AMP/Peer/Presser, 1975). Ives's *114 Songs* will be used as the basic source for songs discussed in this book, even though several of these songs, including "Ann Street," were also published in later song collections that incorporate changes, apparently authorized by Ives, from the musical texts found in *114 Songs.* Since a real critical edition of Ives's songs is as yet unavailable, it seems fruitless here to become embroiled in issues of authenticity and precedence, especially since the variants in the affected songs are almost all of very minor significance; none of the later changes affect any of the issues of style, form, and substance that are under discussion here. The readily available *114 Songs* seems the obvious source of choice, for the sake of consistency, and for the consequent convenience of the reader. It may be assumed that all songs discussed in any detail in these pages may be found in that collection, unless a citation indicates otherwise.

       Throughout these pages on "Ann Street," and at points elsewhere in this book, I am presenting a (Ivesian?) paraphrase of portions of my own article "Style and Substance: 'Ann Street' by Charles Ives," which appeared in *Perspectives of New Music* Vol. 15, No. 2 (Spring-Summer 1977), pp. 23–33. An article covering parallel ground is my "Charles Ives: The Next Hundred Years—Towards a Method of Analysing the Music," in *The Music Review* Vol. 38, No. 2 (May 1977), pp. 101–111. This latter essay used "The Alcotts" movement of Ives's "Concord" Sonata as an analytical case in point.

20   Gunther Schuller's comments are found in the program notes he wrote for the Columbia recording *Calcium Light Night* (MS 7318), which contains twenty short works by Ives performed by a chamber orchestra conducted by Mr. Schuller.

28   Henry and Sidney Cowell's observations are found on p. 144 of their study *Charles Ives and His Music* (New York: Da Capo, 1983).

29   The quotation concerning "Ives's aim" from the Cowells' biography [28] may be found on pp. 173–174.

30   "Seed for next year's planting" is Ives's characterization of an unrelated chord sounded softly over the loud final triad of the song "Luck and Work"; this annotation on his manuscript was referred to by John Kirkpatrick in program notes for a 1974 recording of Ives songs in which Kirkpatrick accompanied soprano Helen Boatwright (part of the Columbia set *Charles Ives: The 100th Anniversary*, M4 32504).

        "The pleasure of never finishing" is a slight paraphrase of the feelings Ives expressed about the "Emerson" movement of the "Concord" Sonata; see Ives's *Memos*, ed. John Kirkpatrick (New York: Norton, 1972), p. 80; see also the Henry and Sidney Cowell biography [28], p. 13.

ANALYSIS AND ITS DISCONTENTS

31–32   "but the greater the distance . . . ": See the conclusion of *Essays Before A Sonata*, in Boatwright [14], p. 102. The ensuing quotations from *Essays Before A Sonata* may be found also in Boatwright on p. 79 ("eclecticism"); p. 94 ("Everyone should have the opportunity"); and p. 14 ("wrings the neck of any law").

32   "*I hear something else!*": See the Cowells' biography [28], p. 70.

32   Kirkpatrick's comments may be found in Perlis's *Charles Ives Remembered* [6], p. 218.

JUXTAPOSITION AND SEQUENCE (II): OTHER TONE ROADS

34   "an exciting, easy and worldly progress . . . ": Ives's remarks on the Fourth Symphony were first conveyed (or paraphrased?) by Henry Bellamann in program notes written for a partial performance of the work in 1927, and these notes have been quoted frequently in the Ives literature. I took my text from the program notes by José Serebrier accompanying the recording of his spectacular performance of this symphony with the London Philharmonic Orchestra (now available on Chandos ABR-1118).

34   Finale of the Fourth Symphony: For Ives's evaluation, see the *Memos* [30], p. 66.

35   Truth as an "activity": See Ives on Emerson in *Essays Before A Sonata* ("He will not accept repose against the activity of truth"), p. 16 in Boatwright [14].

35   "Walking" is song 67 in *114 Songs*.

43   The song "1, 2, 3," No. 41 in *114 Songs*, is derived from some of the music of *Over The Pavements*.

53   *Sixty-Seventh Psalm* is described as an "enlarged plain chant" by Ives in his *Memos* [30]; see pp. 178–179. I discuss this piece in my article "The Early Styles of Charles Ives," in *19th-Century Music* Vol. 7 (Summer 1983), pp. 71–80.

54   New ways to hear traditional works: Lawrence Kramer, in his book, *Music and Poetry: The Nineteenth Century and After* (Berkeley: University of California Press, 1984), offers discussions of instrumental works by Beethoven and Chopin in Chapters 3 and 4, suggesting a stylistic viewpoint toward certain traditional music that is directly compatible with the concerns being explored in this study. Although Kramer also discusses music by Ives in Chapter 6, he does not bring the issue of stylistic change prominently into that discussion. (Kramer

does have some provocative things to say about the matter of quotation in Ives, however; see pp. 175 and 177–178 of the book.)

INFLUENCE

54   For examples of *lieder* in *114 Songs*, see songs 80–83 (No. 82, "Feldeinsamkeit," or "In Summer Fields," is an especially lovely example, which I analyze in my article "The Early Styles of Charles Ives" [53]); songs 76–79 in the collection are French songs; among the best-known songs based on traditional vernacular American styles are "The Circus Band" (song 56) and "Memories" (song 102, also discussed in my article just cited). The two songs from *The Celestial Country* are Nos. 98 and 99. Two examples of songs in internally consistent "modernistic" styles are Nos. 14 ("The Indians") and 64 ("The Cage"); the latter piece will be discussed in Chapter 7.

54   His substance: I am paraphrasing the Ives statement previously quoted on page 17.

55   Ives on Bach and Beethoven: See the *Memos* [30], p. 135.

55   A lack of sufficient stylistic intensity: See the *Memos* [30], pp. 44 and 100.

55   "What my father did for me . . . " is from Ives's *Memos* [30], pp. 114–115. Also see pp. 45–48 in the *Memos* for good examples of Ives's writings about his father. The issues of George Ives's importance and influence in his son's life and musical career have been receiving extensive attention in the scholarly literature. See, as examples of this, Maynard Solomon's article "Charles Ives: Some Questions of Veracity," in the *Journal of the American Musicological Society* Vol. 40, No. 3 (Fall 1987), pp. 443–470; J. Peter Burkholder's "Charles Ives and his Fathers: A Response to Maynard Solomon," in the *Institute for Studies in American Music Newsletter* Vol. 18, No. 1 (November 1988), pp. 8–11; and Stuart Feder's articles "Charles and George Ives: The Veneration of Boyhood," in *The Annual of Psychoanalysis* Vol. 9 (1981), pp. 265–316, and "Charles Ives and the Unanswered Question," in *The Psychoanalytic Study of Society* Vol. 10, ed. Munsterberger, Boyer, and Grolnick (Hillsdale, NJ and London: The Analytic Press, 1984), pp. 321–351. (The article by Feder on "Decoration Day," cited below [103], also deals at length with the relationship between George and Charles Ives.)

MENTAL JOURNEYS (1)

57   "something that happens . . . " is from the "Hawthorne" essay in Ives's *Essays Before A Sonata;* see Boatwright [14], p. 42.

58   On dissonance and masculinity in Ives's aesthetic thought, see Frank R. Rossiter's *Charles Ives and His America* (New York: Liveright, 1975), pp. 36–37 (and many other passages *passim*).

58   "The Things Our Fathers Loved" is song 43 in *114 Songs*. For a discussion of this song, which emphasizes psychological issues and Ives's use of quotations, see Stuart Feder's article "The Nostalgia of Charles Ives: An Essay in Affects and Music," in *The Annual of Psychoanalysis* Vol. 10 (1982), pp. 301–332.

67   "where new horizons wait" is from the ending of the Robert Underwood

Johnson poem "Premonitions," used by Ives as the text for song 24 in *114 Songs*.

TRADITIONALISM AND MODERNISM

68   Traditionalism: the definition given is also from *Webster's Ninth New Collegiate Dictionary* (1987).

70   The Copland quotation is from "The Ives Case," a chapter in his book *The New Music: 1900–1960*, revised and enlarged edition (New York: Norton, 1968), p. 117. The whole passage deserves to be quoted, as an illustration of Copland's inspiring critical insight and ability to render just praise to another composer: "I myself was guilty of a . . . misapprehension . . . when I said that Ives 'could not organize his material, particularly in his larger works, so that we come away with a unified impression.' His complexities don't always add up, but when they do, a richness of experience is suggested that is unobtainable in any other way. For Ives it was a triumph of daring, a gamble with the future that he has miraculously won."

MENTAL JOURNEYS (II)

71   "Tom Sails Away" is song 51 in *114 Songs*.

QUOTATION

78   On Ives's use of quotation to create internal relationships in his music, see J. Peter Burkholder's article "'Quotation' and Emulation: Charles Ives's Uses of His Models," in *The Musical Quarterly* Vol. 71, No. 1 (1985), pp. 1–26.

78   Scholars engaged in identifying Ives's quoted tunes: See especially Clayton W. Henderson's *The Charles Ives Tunebook* (Michigan: Harmonie Park Press, 1990) for the most recent and thoroughgoing scholarly effort of this kind.

79   " . . . if local color . . . " may be found in Boatwright [14], p. 81.

79   "unprotected from all the showers of the absolute" is another phrase I have borrowed from the epilogue to *Essays Before A Sonata;* see Boatwright [14], p. 92.

JUXTAPOSITION AND SEQUENCE (III): SOME SUMMARIZING WORKS

80   The works discussed in this chapter: *Psalm 90* was published by Merion in 1970; "On The Antipodes" and "General William Booth Enters Into Heaven" are in *19 Songs* (Merion); a new Ives Society edition of "Decoration Day" was published by Peer in 1989.

92   Observers of Ives's music: "On The Antipodes" is discussed in "A Digest Analysis of Ives' 'On The Antipodes'" (notes on a lecture by Dominick Argento) in *Student Musicologists at Minnesota* Vol. 6 (1975–1976), pp. 192–200, and in Chapter 10 of J. Peter Burkholder's unpublished dissertation "The Evolution of Charles Ives's Music: Aesthetics, Quotation, Technique" (University of Chicago, 1983). The "waves" of density and registral patterns are analyzed by Burkholder.

93   Ruggles is quoted in Perlis's *Charles Ives Remembered: An Oral History* [6], p. 176.

159

The George Ives remark may be found on p. 24 of the Cowells' biography [28]; also see Ives's *Memos* [30], p. 132.

103   A work that has received much discussion: See especially Stuart Feder's "Decoration Day: A Boyhood Memory of Charles Ives," *The Musical Quarterly* Vol. 66, No. 2 (1980), pp. 234–261.

106   "Taps:" This is arguably the only quotation in the piece a modern listener is likely to recognize unaided. The recognition will reinforce Ives's program for the piece, but the stylistic logic and function of this transition passage is evident irrespective of the issue of identifying the tune. This is especially true because the melody of Reeves's march in Section 3 is also built directly from the notes of an arpeggiated major triad, presented in the same relative order as in "Taps," although much more quickly. The point I wish to stress here is that, from a purely *musical* standpoint, the stylistic functions and the interrelationships of Ives's quotations are readily grasped by the listener and offer sufficient and convincing rationale for their employment.
The one additional quotation mentioned specifically in Ives's program note for "Decoration Day" is "Adeste Fideles" ("O come, all ye faithful"—although, as Paul C. Echols points out in his notes accompanying the Michael Tilson Thomas performance, the tune was associated with a different text in Ives's youth), which forms the basis for the flowing melody of Section 2. This quotation could escape the listener's notice, even if he knows "Adeste Fideles" well, since Ives presents his melody so slowly and alters so many of the quoted tune's intervals. Actually, Ives is "paraphrasing" rather than quoting here, to use J. Peter Burkholder's term; see Burkholder's article on quotation [78]. Again, the reason for the "paraphrase" is best understood in stylistic terms: Ives is moving closer to a traditional style in Section 2, but he also wants to maintain a certain distance from tradition and familiarity here. Without that distance, the sense of gradual stylistic progression would not emerge in the piece, and the special impact of Section 3 and its C–major outburst would be diluted.

109   Ives's program: The program is quoted in full in *Memos* [30], pp. 101–102, footnote 1, and on p. 33 of the published score [80].

PERFORMANCE, PROFESSIONALISM, AND AMATEURS

110   On amateur music-making: For one of the best of Ives's celebrations of this, see the *Memos* [30], pp. 132–133.

110   "You won't get a heroic ride to Heaven . . . ": I am once again quoting George Ives. See the note for page 93.

111   On "piano-drum" chords, see the *Memos* [30], pp. 42–43.

111   The Cowells' account of Slonimsky's 1931 performance is in their *Charles Ives and His Music* [28], p. 106.

112   "Charlie Rutlage" is song 10 in *114 Songs*.

LAYERING

116   "The Housatonic at Stockbridge" is song 15 in *114 Songs*.

116   Inconsistent spelling of pitches: Some, but not all, of the spelling idiosyncracies in "The Housatonic at Stockbridge" may be explained by the probability that

Ives worked directly from his earlier orchestral score when notating the version for voice and piano. The notation of the voice in D♭, rather than C♯, major certainly reflects the original orchestral source, where the melody later given to the voice is played alternately by the French horn and the English horn—instruments in F whose music reads much more easily when the notation is in flat rather than sharp keys. In the song, the occurrences of F♮ both in the vocal part and in the left hand of the piano point up occasional "common tone" relationships between these lines and the other stylistic layer in the piece, since F♮ is a recurring pitch in the right hand of the piano as well.

125   ". . . why tonality as such . . . " is from Ives's essay, "Some 'Quarter-Tone' Impressions"; see Boatwright [14], p. 117.

126   "good place to stop, not end" is what Ives wrote at the end of his sketch for the second movement of his Second String Quartet. See John Kirkpatrick's *A Temporary Mimeographed Catalogue of the Music Manuscripts and Related Materials of Charles Edward Ives, 1874–1954* (New Haven: Library of the Yale School of Music, 1960), p. 60.

126   "The Cage" is No. 64 in *114 Songs*.

SONG

130   Ives's earliest and last works: *Psalm 42* and the song "Slow March" (the "last" of the *114 Songs*) were both written before Ives was fourteen; "Sunrise," from 1926, and the arrangement of the spiritual "In the Mornin'," from 1929, are the last completed works.

THE STRUCTURING OF STYLES: ADDITIONAL ALTERNATIVES

132   "good place to stop, not end": See the note for page 126.

133   "give all the 'old girls' another ride": See the *Memos* [30], p. 127.

139   "Maple Leaves" is song 23 in *114 Songs*.

141   "Remembrance" and "The Pond" have been discussed by Stuart Feder; see especially his article "Charles Ives and the Unanswered Question" [55], pp. 336–339 and 345.

PERFECTIONISM AND "SERENITY"

143   "Serenity" is song 42 in *114 Songs*. For other discussions of "Serenity," see Burkholder's article on quotation [78], pp. 11–13, and Douglass M. Green's "A Chord Motive in Ives's 'Serenity,'" *In Theory Only* Vol. 4, No. 5 (October 1978), pp. 20–21.

143   Ives's *Memos* indicate: See p. 126 in the *Memos* [30].

148   The Walt Whitman excerpt is from stanza 51 of *Song of Myself*. Eric Salzman points out the kinship between Whitman and Ives in his *Twentieth-Century Music: An Introduction,* third edition (Englewood Cliffs: Prentice-Hall, 1988), p. 135.

POSTLUDE

150   It is hard to be entirely comfortable with this: Salzman's *Twentieth-Century Music: An Introduction* [148] deserves to be cited again here. See his remark

about Ives on p. 136: "This is more than just composing unusual music; it is a change in the meaning of the act of composing itself."

150   "activity of truth": See the note for page 35.

153   "There is always something more to be said": See the Cowells' biography [28], p. viii.

A Discographical Note

Much of Ives's output is readily available on recordings, and there seems no need to provide a comprehensive listing of the recorded works of Ives here. What I do want to offer the reader is a very brief guide to current recordings of the songs discussed in detail in this book, especially since these songs are spread out among several song collections, not one of which contains them all.

For obvious reasons, I will limit my discussion to cassettes and compact discs in current catalogs at the time of this writing (January, 1991). Unfortunately, some excellent recordings of songs by Ives have long been unavailable for purchase. (Those readers with access to good music libraries may still be able to hear important rarities like the 1954 Overtone recording of an Ives song recital by Helen Boatwright, soprano, and John Kirkpatrick, pianist.) But those who choose from what is presently available have some enviable options.

In my view, the late Jan DeGaetani was without peer as an interpreter of Ives's vocal music, and her collaborations with pianist Gilbert Kalish have set the standards by which all performances of Ives's songs will be judged for the foreseeable future. The DeGaetani-Kalish collection of Ives songs on Nonesuch 71325 is the recording of choice for those seeking an introduction to this literature. It contains seventeen songs, including "Ann Street," "The Things Our Fathers Loved," "The Housatonic at Stockbridge," "The Cage," "Majority," and "Serenity." A later recording by DeGaetani and Kalish for the Bridge label, presenting music by Ives and Crumb, is now available on compact disc (# 9006); it offers nine Ives songs, including "Tom Sails Away."

Soprano Roberta Alexander and pianist Tan Crone have released two volumes of Ives songs on the Etcetera label. The first, on Etcetera 1020, contains (among many others) "The Things Our Fathers Loved," "Tom Sails Away," "Charlie Rutlage," "The Housatonic at Stockbridge," "The Cage," "Maple Leaves," and "Serenity"; the second, available only on compact disc (Etcetera 1068), contains "Ann Street" and "Remembrance." Alexander obviously loves this repertoire, and her performances are estimable, both careful and caring, even if some of them seem rather mannered when compared with those of DeGaetani.

Both historical importance and aesthetic interest are to be found in the early recordings of Ives songs made in the 1930s for Henry Cowell's *New Music Quarterly*, which have been reissued by Composers Recordings, Inc., on CRI 6014 (cassette only). This reissue offers a spirited rendition of "General William Booth Enters Into Heaven" by soprano Radiana Pazmor and pianist Genevieve Pitot, as well as six other songs, including "Ann Street" and "Charlie Rutlage," performed by Mordecai Bauman, baritone, accompanied by Albert Hirsh.

This leaves "Walking" and "On The Antipodes." "Walking" may be heard in a Carolyn Watkinson recital on Etcetera 1007 (cassette only), which also includes "Tom Sails Away" and "The Cage," two other Ives songs, and works by several other composers; the contralto is accompanied by Tan Crone. Lamentably, but unsurprisingly, there is at present no available recording of "On The Antipodes"; I hope that some fearless musicians will attempt to close this lacuna within my lifetime. I should also note here that *Psalm 90* is disappointingly absent from the current catalogs. But the production of compact discs is moving forward so intensively that I fully expect this last observation, at least, to be out of date by the time this book is published, or shortly thereafter. It should not be long before there are many more fine performances of Ives's vocal music available to satisfy the curiosity and needs of both casual listeners and connoisseurs of twentieth-century music.

Index of Musical Compositions

All works are by Charles Ives, unless indicated otherwise. Page numbers in **boldface** indicate extended discussions of works, with accompanying musical examples or illustrative tables.

"America," Variations on. *See* Variations on "America"

Ann Street, 5, **20–30,** 33, 34, 35, 36, 41, 42, 43, 58, 75, 104, 133

Browning Overture, 129

Cage, The, 35, 67, **126–129**

Calcium Light Night, 34

Call of the Mountains, The. *See* String Quartet No. 2

Celestial Country, The, 54

Central Park in the Dark, 69, 116, 126

Charlie Rutlage, **112–113**

Circus Band, The, 34, 69

"Concord" Sonata. *See* Piano Sonata No. 2

Decoration Day. *See under* Symphony: New England Holidays

Double Concerto for Piano and Harpsichord (Carter), 14

Down East, 138

Ein musikalischer Spass (Mozart). *See* A Musical Joke

"Eroica" Symphony (Beethoven). *See* Symphony No. 3

Farewell to Land, A, 34

Fountain (Mason), quoted by Ives, 93–95

Fourth of July, The. *See under* Symphony: New England Holidays

From Hanover Square North, at the End of a Tragic Day, the Voice of the People Again Arose. *See* Orchestral Set No. 2

From "Paracelsus," 129

165

Index of Names

DATE DUE

GAYLORD   PRINTED IN U.S.A.